Er. M.K. Gupta

How to Remain Ever Happy

Release stress & anxiety and live life with joy & happiness

PUSTAK MAHAL®

Published by
Pustak Mahal®

Administrative office and Sales Centre
J-3/16, Daryaganj, New Delhi-110002
☎ 011-23276539, 23272783, 23272784, 23260518
E-mail: info@pustakmahal.com • *Website:* www.pustakmahal.com

Branch Office
Bengaluru: ☎ 080-22234025, 40912845
E-mail: pustakmahalblr@gmail.com

ISBN 978-81-223-0047-5
Edition: 2025

Printed at : Glorious Printers, Delhi

Preface

There was no great planning of writing this book since I have been mostly interested in reading the books rather than writing. My interest in reading has been mostly centred around knowing the truths and mysteries of life and discovering the ways to eternal happiness with consequent removal of miseries and sufferings which an ordinary man normally undergoes in life. I do not hesitate to disclose here that by now, I must have read thousands of books relating to *yoga*, spirituality, human mind and also on health-care. There is nothing great in it. It is only a question of interest.

It suddenly dawned on me as to why not crystallize some of these ideas floating in my mind into a concise, simple and systematic form which may be easily assimilated and applied into practice by a common man. This is how the pen started and when it stopped, I found that this has become a book in itself. As I started writing, more and more ideas started pouring in. To give the ideas a proper shape in the form of a presentable book, lot of resetting, modifications, typing, retyping and all that labour which is required for making a presentable book, was done. Now the fruits of this labour are in your hands. I will consider this labour well spent if the book proves to be of some value to you. After all, the final evaluation of the ideas and wisdom of the book lies in the hands of the readers only.

The writings contained herein are not only based on my study of innumerable books but are also corroborated by my personal experiences and realizations in life. I request the readers not to read this book casually like a cheap novel. Read it not in hurry but when you are at leisure and at peace, free from disturbances and distractions.

For the benefit of my readers, I have also given references of my other books at appropriate places for those who want to go into more details about a particular topic.

I may also inform my readers that now this book has been published in many languages. While Hindi and Bangla editions have been brought out by the same publisher, the other language editions have been published by other publishers, the details of which can be had from the author/publisher.

I would also like to give a good news to my readers that I have written one more book in the similar pattern as the present book titled ***'77 Lessons to Remain Ever Positive.'*** Those who wish to learn more about the realities and truths of life may love to read this book.

I am open to any comments/suggestions by the readers and also to any further clarifications sought by an inquisitive reader which can be conveyed to me without any hesitation.

May you enjoy and benefit from the book.

New Delhi

—Er. M.K. Gupta

E-mail: *mkg@iuac.ernet.in*

Contents

Few quotes on happiness

- Happiness is a state of mind, it doesn't reside in a place or in a situation or in an object.
- Nobody can make you happy except you yourself.
- Money can give you everything except happiness.
- Happiness can't be purchased. It can only be experienced.
- Fountain of happiness is inside you. Don't make futile attempts to search it outside.
- Even if you are made the king of the whole world and are handed over all the possessions and objects of pleasure, there is no guarantee that you will be happy.
- Happiness is your true intrinsic nature. It is only to be discovered and not to be acquired from outside.
- The origin of stress is in your mind. Without understanding and controlling the mind, it is impossible to eliminate stress.
- Nobody can make you unhappy unless you allow him to do so.
- Happiness is your valuable treasure. Don't allow it to be snatched by varying circumstances and petty matters of life.
- Happiness is measured by the spirit with which you face the problems of life.
- To seek happiness outside is like trying to lasso a cloud.
- Happiness does not come from doing what we like to do but from liking what we have to do.
- Happiness is found in little things: a baby's smile, a letter from a friend, the song of a bird, the sunlight through the window.

- Happiness is like perfume; you can't spray it on others without getting some on yourself.
- Happiness grows out of harmonious relationships with others, based on attitudes of goodwill, tolerance, understanding and love.
- We are as happy as we make ourselves so.
- Happiness comes upon you unaware while you help others. *'Help thy brother's boat across, and lo! thine own has reached the shore too'.*
- The best way to keep others happy is to ensure that you are happy.
- Tension or unhappiness is not an object or a thing or a situation. It is our reaction towards a thing or a situation, which generates it.
- Happiness doesn't come from the fulfilment of desires but from the cessation of desires.
- If more number of people desired their own happiness more than they desired the unhappiness of others, we could have paradise on earth very shortly.
- Happiness: It is such a treasure—I would buy it, beg it, steal it, fight for it and die for it.
- Happiness will never come to those who fail to appreciate what they already have.
- Where comparison and competition ends, happiness begins.
- The foolish man seeks happiness in the distance, the wise searches it inside, in the centre of his being.
- The secret of happiness is freedom and the secret of freedom, courage.

What is happiness?

Before embarking upon a detailed discussion on this fascinating topic, we have to first appreciate this fact greatly in our mind that happiness and unhappiness are basically states of mind and are not necessarily dependent on outer circumstances and conditions. In other words, ***they come from inside and not from outside***. For example, two persons can react very differently in the same situation. While one can become highly tense and anxious, other can still maintain a state of calmness and happiness while dealing with the situation.

Hence what determines our happiness or unhappiness is not the external circumstances or conditions but our mental attitude or reaction towards those circumstances. It will not be an exaggeration to say that ***mental attitude is everything in life***. Various religions have pointed out towards a reservoir of joy, happiness, love, peace, strength and wisdom existing inside us. It has been variously called by different religions as your ***'Divine Self'*** or ***'Inner Self'*** or ***'Real Self'*** or ***'Spirit'*** or ***'Divine Spark'*** or ***'Innermost being'*** etc. This is where we have to gain access to get true happiness. And you can see that this source is nowhere else except inside you. By changing our mental attitudes in a positive manner, we come nearer and nearer to this source.

Therefore, to remain ever happy, what we have to do is just readjustment of our mental attitudes. That is all in a nutshell. To readjust our mental attitudes, we need knowledge of life and an increase in our mental strength and will-power. In this book, I am giving some tips for changing your mental attitudes and increasing the strength and will-power of your mind, which if you incorporate in your everyday life, will lead to eternal happiness, peace and stability of mind.

I have chosen a very practical way of explaining and also layman's expressions and language, so that you can just flow with the writing without trapping yourself in mind-boggling technicalities and philosophy. Please note that these are not mere theoretical preachings. They have been tested and experienced practically, by innumerable persons in the past who had the key to eternal happiness. You are advised to read it over and over again and alongwith contemplation on each point after reading, to derive the maximum benefit from it and to get the points properly settled in your mind.

If I wait to be happy
I will wait forever
If I am happy now
I will be happy forever

1. Concentration

As physical exercises strengthen the body, concentration increases the strength of mind. Strong mind is not easily affected or disturbed by trials and tribulations of life. For improving concentration whatever activity we may be engaged in, we should try to be totally absorbed in it, however trivial it may be. At that time, except this activity (and associated things) the whole world should be dead for us. For example, even if we are eating a fruit at a moment, we should completely relish each morsel of fruit with our attention totally dedicated to it. If we are bathing, we should relish this activity fully, deriving maximum benefit from it by keeping our attention totally anchored to it. If you are reading a book, be totally absorbed in it for that time oblivious of any other thing. You should learn to concentrate on uninteresting things also to develop real control of mind.

Concentration, in other words, means to learn to remain in the present moment which is the most desirable feature for success and happiness in life.

2. Detachment and letting go

Alongwith concentration, we should also develop the ability to detach ourselves from any thing or task at a moment's notice. Some people can concentrate and absorb in a task, but, they find it difficult to forget this first activity completely while taking on to the next activity. They have some hangover period. This only shows that we get unduly attached towards various things which actually we should not.

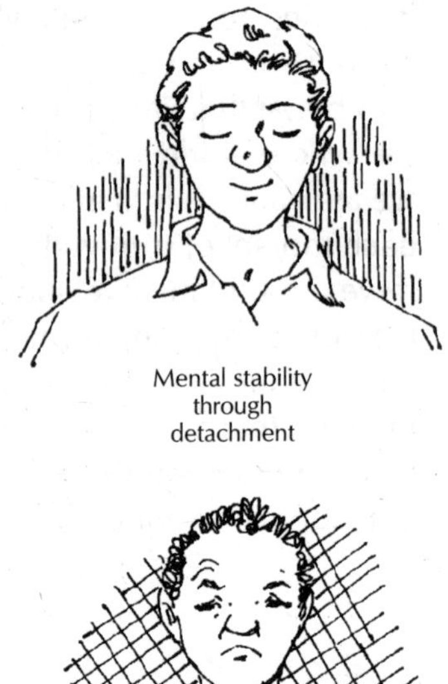

Mental stability through detachment

Mental tension with attachment

Please note that the world is a great training school. **The only importance of various worldly things and incidents is to give us necessary training and lessons for our growth.** ***They themselves are not important as such.*** Hence, we should only use them for our learning and growth, but, not get overly attached to them and once the purpose is served by learning necessary lesson, we should forget and discard them. **Concentration and detachment should be practised simultaneously.** This is what Swami Vivekananda also emphasized a lot. Ability to forget and detach from past is a great quality for achieving success in life. It is well said ***'Though it is sometimes useful to remember, but it is often wise to forget'.***

Note: Strictly speaking, nothing is forgotten, everything gets stored in our subconscious mind; what we mean by the word 'forgetting' here is that we should not consciously bring that thing to our mind again and again.

3. Planned thinking

Ensure at various intervals that your thinking is planned and systematic and not haphazard and random. Unplanned random thinking, day dreaming is a sign of weak mind and indicates that instead of controlling your subconscious mind, (that part of mind where all your urges, desires, inclinations lie stored) you are being controlled by it. Your conscious mind should remain fully active, in full awareness and maintain its master status controlling its servant (subconscious mind). By going into passive, idle and day dreaming state, you encourage the influence of subconscious mind over your conscious mind. So ensure that only those thoughts are in your mind which you really want to have at that moment. It has been noted in a survey that a sizable portion of one's life time is spent in wasteful thinking. This can be easily channeled for performing useful activities.

Note: To understand more about the functioning of conscious mind and subconscious mind, please refer my book **'How to Control Mind and be Stress-free'**.

4. Positive thinking

We give the least importance to this most important aspect of our life i.e. how we think. It is the single largest factor in building up of our personality and character. Develop the habit of viewing everything positively, even the most miserable situations. Negative thinking weakens the mind, makes it restless, agitated and impure. Convert every negative situation into positive one by readjusting your mental attitude. To quote an example as to how it should be done, suppose, someone abuses you or makes undesirable remarks in anger, then instead of feeling bad about him, just think that his mood is upset or he is still not fully mature; that is why he is saying this. But, don't develop any malice against him. This is positive attitude.

By having positive thinking, you will also attract to yourself favourable physical conditions and environment because by the law of psychic attraction, you attract physical conditions and circumstances towards you according to your thoughts. For example, suppose you repeatedly develop a fearful thought that you may catch a particular disease, you will find subsequently that symptoms of the same disease start occurring in you. ***Such is the power of thoughts. They are as real as a solid stone.***

By remaining positive, you create an aura of positive vibrations around you which not only benefit you, but, all others coming into contact with you. This aura also protects you from the attack of any negativity released by others.

Note: For greater understanding of the nature & effect of thoughts and operation of conscious & subconscious minds, please refer my book **'How to Control Mind and be Stress-free'**.

5. Reduce emotional involvement, take things easy

The root cause of our suffering is our emotional involvement while dealing with various incidents, situations and circumstances of life. We should watch and tackle all worldly objects and situations objectively like a spectator as if they are different and we are different and we only have a temporary association with them.

The cause of our emotional involvement with worldly things is that we are taking them too seriously which actually we should not. ***We should realise that no difficulties or problems are permanent. They all will pass. Such is the law. Everything is in a state of constant motion and change. Nothing is permanent and static here.***

Taking things seriously also results in formation of deep impressions *(samskaras)* in your subconscious mind which results in development of various biases and prejudices in our mind in favour of and against various things and reduces its ability to see things objectively (i.e. as they really are). In other words, emotions of like, dislike, love, hatred, jealousy, revenge etc. should be gradually rooted out resulting in a truly unbiased and detached mind which can remain calm, serene and balanced in all the trials and odds of life.

6. Welcome difficulties and problems of life, they are for our good

Regarding various problems, pains and discomforts which we face in life, we should try to develop the philosophy that these have not come to us for frightening. In fact these pains and discomforts are the very things we need at this moment to strengthen and grow wherever we are lacking. They are the trials and tests for us. Instead of opposing them, we should, at such occasions stop for a while, do some self-evaluation and introspection and learn the needed lesson from them. ***We can derive some benefit and learning from every problem or difficulty of life and exploit it to our advantage. This is a wonderful law of life.*** In every adversity and difficulty, ask yourself what message this problem has brought for me and what benefit I can derive from it. You must come out wiser and more mature after going through a problem.

If we fight with these discomforts and accuse ourselves and others, we are simply invoking a new chain of cause and effect and making matters worse. Remember that ***everything which happens to us in life is for our good only. In the***

***apparently looking cruel and adverse circumstances is hidden the infinite mercy of* God** which we can realise if we properly contemplate upon it. That is why enlightened persons always thank God in problems and consider them as *'Prasad'* of God. They never question God, but, simply flow with His decisions accepting everything and avoiding nothing.

You have been placed by* God *exactly where you deserve. This placing is actually needed by you for your growth or for working out or balancing some *karmas*. ***Once you play your present role successfully, you will be automatically shifted to the next higher place.***

7. There is a reason for everything, nothing happens by chance or accident

Remember that there is a reason for everything which happens. Nothing happens by chance or accident. ***Universe has a certain order and everything is bound by a relationship of cause and effect. For every effect there is a cause.*** Whatever is happening to you right now is because you have put certain causes into operation in the past and unless all those causes are gradually worked out in the form of effects and no fresh causes are generated by us, we will not be free and happy for ever.

Based on the above knowledge, change your mental attitude in confronting various incidents and problems of life. Don't view them as burden coming to you out of nowhere. Consider all problems as projects and as means to grow and ***remain even minded in success/failure, gain/loss, praise/insult so as to stop any fresh bondage of karma. It is not the incidents or events which are important, but, our mental attitude and reaction towards them.*** That is why it has been aptly said that ***'World is neither good nor bad. It depends upon how we look at it'*** or in other words, it depends on the state of our mind. ***Whatever is within us, same appears to us outside.***

8. Silence, solitude and self-introspection

Try to find some time daily when you are in solitude and in silence and devote this time solely for yourself. Try to do some self-introspection in this time as to in which areas you need improvements and strengthening, in which areas you are slipping. By this self analysis give necessary suggestions to yourself to improve.

Through silence you conserve mental energy. Always speak less, speak in low and sweet voice and to the point. Never talk too much and in high pitch. Avoid gossips, unnecessary arguments and discussions. ***There should always be some aim when you talk. Aimless talking should always be avoided.*** Much physical and mental energy is wasted in useless discussions.

9. Overcome fears

Fears are a drain on our mental energy and are main stumbling blocks to our progress. ***By the law of attraction, whatever we fear or doubt, we actually attract those conditions*** and circumstances around us and so we are further trapped in a vicious circle. There are some people among us who constantly fear lest this or that should happen and thus keep their minds constantly in a state of agitation and turmoil.

Please remember there is nothing in this world which we really need to fear. Nothing is designed in the Universe to harm us. One of the best ways to remove fear is to intentionally face and stand before those very things you fear denying mentally that they can do any harm to you, till such time when the fear is totally gone. The causes of your fear leap on you again and again until you overcome fear. It is a law that the more you fear a thing, the more it frightens you. However, if you don't fear and stand before it untouched and indifferent, the opposite happens i.e. the fear will go away from you. ***Also bear in mind this great truth that actual mishappening is never that fearful and painful as our thought or imagination of that happening.***

Even incidents of so called ghosts, black magic, soul possession and various other para-psychical influences affect only those persons who are mentally fearful, weak and remain sensitive to these things. These things can't touch a strong-minded person.

Further, also gain strength by the knowledge (as has been explained earlier) that nothing happens by chance or by accident. For every happening there is a reason. Hence, why the fear of anything suddenly happening to you. Just face each challenge of life boldly with positive outlook and firm faith in God who only can provide the real security to us.

Note: For greater understanding of physiology and psychology of fear, please refer my book **'How to Overcome Fear'**.

10. Don't have inferiority complex, what others can do, you can also do

Many people have inferiority complex that they can't do certain things which others can. They don't have confidence in their calibre and capability. Please remember that ultimate potential of all of us is exactly the same. No one is any better or worse than us provided we can explore the potential of our mind through meditation and soul consciousness. The reason being that all souls are exactly same as far as their original attributes are concerned. There is not even an iota of difference. ***Hence never compare with others and neither feel inferior nor feel superior to anybody.***

Have full confidence that whatever others can do, you can also do. It is only a question of awakening of your dormant mental faculties. In fact, there is no problem which we can't solve by developing our mind fully and if we can put our developed mind always attuned to God (our spiritual Father), we can then even share the vast powers of our Father (God) also.

11. Don't waste time

Normally it is seen that although we are running around here & there a lot, but, without any concrete output. In short, we are simply dissipating our energy. Life is short and very precious. Time is running very fast. ***Every moment we are coming closer to death. It can fall at any moment without any notice.*** Hence, don't waste any time here. We have to achieve maximum in this minimum time. Ensure that each moment we are progressing onwards and not shifting backwards. Don't waste your time in useless thinking, gossips and loitering here and there. Time which has been lost by you is lost for ever and can't be regained by you by any means. Time, like any other commodity, can't be stored. Time not utilized is wasted for ever. There is a saying: ***'Waste your money and you are only out of money, but, waste your time and you have lost a part of your life.'*** Hence, always be busy in some useful constructive work.

Many people don't realize how they are wasting their precious life time

Whatever profession or activity you are involved in in your life, explore the techniques that you may get maximum output with minimum expenditure of time and energy. Always ask yourself whether the amount of time and energy you are spending on a particular work is really worth. Are you not spending more time and energy than what is required? Your input of time energy and the output you get must be in proportion. Learn time management for achieving maximum efficiency and optimum utilization of your efforts and energy. Also study human psychology for efficient interaction with your colleagues, superiors and juniors and for getting best out of them with least friction and least expenditure of energy. Plan your works, list down your priorities and follow a systematic approach instead of carrying on at random as most people do.

Please remember that ***we are answerable to our Father (God) for each and everything we are doing on this earth plane (including thinking, speaking)*** and all these have a very great impact on our future fate and next life.

12. Control over impulses, observe self-restraint and patience

In your daily life, just don't follow your impulses and start doing or saying anything whichever comes to your mind. It is a sign of weak mind. Have some checks and controls on your mind and never become its slave. Be the master of your mind and senses. Let them (mind and senses) work as your servant and they should not be allowed to cross their limits. Your intellect in association with your conscience should maintain its superiority over these lower faculties. Whatever impulse or urge comes in your mind (it comes from your subconscious mind where these tendencies, desires, passions lie in dormant state), don't jump over it immediately. First examine it properly and then accordingly hold it for sometime or ignore it totally. ***By exercising patience in this manner your will-power and mental strength will increase gradually*** which is a necessary prerequisite for a satisfying and contented life.

To quote an example: suppose, it suddenly comes to your mind that you should eat *Golgappa* or *Chat*. In such a state of your desire, there are two courses open to you. One is to rush immediately and satisfy your lust, another is to hold a check on your mind and examine by intellect how much reasonable it would be to rush instantly to a few miles. By adopting second course, you increase your will-power. You should try to exercise such type of patience everywhere and avoid hurry, anxiety and desperation for worldly matters and sensual pleasures. ***Only area where impatience is allowed is in finding God.***

Power of a controlled mind increases in the same fashion as the power of water increases when it is controlled and channeled by constructing a dam.

13. Don't react immediately when provoked

Whenever you feel disturbed or restless due to some sudden problems or some irrelevant remarks or comments by somebody, avoid reacting immediately or coming under sudden provocation. Allow sometime to pass and refrain from doing or saying anything as long as disturbance persists in your mind. It is best if you temporarily avoid the person or situation whom you consider the cause of your disturbance. Preferably go away from that place and sit silently in solitude for sometime. Slow down and cool down yourself and then examine coolly all pros and cons. You are most likely to understand better about the real problem in this state of mind. ***Under provocation, the reasoning power of the mind gets destroyed.***

Give clarifications to people of your innocence only when asked for. Don't force your innocence on people. Your voice in reply should always be polite, respectful and controlled. You should never behave in an uncontrolled fashion and not resort to shouting while replying, howsoever wrong blame or criticism has been done to you.

14. Brooding over past and worrying for future

Some people practically waste their whole lives on these two occupations. It is possible that you couldn't do what you should have done in the past. But, to spoil the present because of that is also not wise. Similarly spoiling our present by worrying for future which we can't foresee right now, is also not wise. In fact, by spoiling our present by the above two operations, we are deliberately spoiling our future also.

Please remember that ***present is the most important moment of your life. What matters most to you and to the world right now is what you are at present and not what you were or what you will be.*** Nobody is going to bother about your past problems and situations and is also not going to favour you in employment or in an examination just because you had so and so problems in the past. They are only interested in what you are at present. So take proper hold of your present. By taking control of the present we can not only lay a good foundation for our future, but, can even reduce the effect of past *karmic* bondages considerably.

Past should be used only for learning some lessons from it so that these mistakes are not repeated. Besides this there is no importance of past. Just forget it like an old movie witnessed by you. There is no dearth of opportunities in our life to progress. If you have lost some opportunities in the past, you can still catch the train now. Opportunities of all sorts are always there before us. Only we should have the necessary will or desire to grab them.

15. You are the master of your destiny

To those people who always start cursing their luck while they face misfortunes, please remember that ***you are hundred percent responsible for what you are in your life. You have made your destiny by your own hands.*** Your past has made your present. Your present will make your future. What you are experiencing today is the fruits of what you have done in the past. Future is still in your hands if you are cautious enough to keep your present in order. Hence, never curse your luck for misfortunes, but, face the reality boldly. ***Accepting self responsibility for your life and the realization that your thoughts, words and actions are the mould for shaping your future, can bring about a major change in your attitude towards life.***

Further, you have a power with you by which you can even modify and alter your present destiny also. You needn't be helpless slave in the hands of destiny. By exercising positive thinking and making actual physical efforts with firm determination and will-power against various obstacles, you can defeat the forces of destiny. If you can also surrender yourself to God, then it becomes further easier to detach from the wheel of destiny because of divine help available to you at every step.

Thus, it is not necessary to revolve endlessly in the wheel of destiny like a galley slave. You have the power to come out of this wheel and control it instead of being controlled by it. ***As your level of consciousness rises, the hold of the destiny over you gets weakened.*** That is why spiritually enlightened persons are not afraid of destiny at all. They are at a level where they are not moved by the things, but, they themselves move the things. They have the handle of the wheel of destiny in their hands by which they can change the fixed conditions. Destiny works as their servant unlike all of us where destiny works as a master and we act as its servants.

There is another dimension to it also. Once you achieve a higher level of consciousness and mental control, you don't get affected by adverse destiny. You can withstand it calmly instead of breaking down as happens with a weak-minded person. Your reaction and attitude towards adversities of life totally changes. You don't take them seriously and don't

question them. You realise that they have come in accordance with certain law and will also disappear after sometimes according to the same law. Thus, by detaching yourself and by stepping back and looking at all these adversities like an observer, you remain mentally stable. It is only in the mind where you feel all sorts of pains, frustrations, worries, anxieties, fears etc. Once you control your mind, all these circumstances will lose hold on you and will surrender at your feet.

Note: For greater understanding of the operation of Destiny & Freewill in our life, please read the article **'Destiny and Freewill'** in my book **'How to Control Mind and be Stress-free'.**

16. Self-satisfaction before satisfaction of others

Many people live a life style which is primarily aimed at impressing and satisfying others. They give more importance to what people think about them than what they think about themselves. This is one of the main reasons for our frustrations in life. Please note that ***it is more important for you as to what you think about yourselves than what others think.*** Your self analysis about you is much more important. Nobody knows you better than you yourself. Hence, don't get straightway carried away by the judgement or opinion of others about you whether it be your praise or criticism. Weigh them with your intellect and then accept only those remarks which you consider appropriate. Other people's judgement about you is not necessarily a correct one because it is according to their mental biases. ***Only an enlightened person who has remained very close to you can give a correct judgment about you.***

Always be in your natural state with a simple and decent life style irrespective of what others think about you and don't try to artificially influence people. ***Trying to pretend what you are not is one of the greatest sources of stress.***

17. Accept and recognise your weaknesses

Once you have recognised your weaknesses, you have already taken the first step in removing them. There should be no hesitation in accepting your weaknesses before others and there should be no attempt to hide them because it is natural for all human beings to have some or the other weaknesses and to commit mistakes.

What is important is that after recognizing your weakness, you should start making efforts to eradicate it. This is what makes us humane and distinct from animal species.

If you feel that by knowing your weaknesses other people will think low of you, then, ***remember that it is always better to be recognised less than what you actually are*** because then you don't have to strain every time to prove yourself upto other people's expectations. Moreover, as explained earlier, it is not important what people think about you, but, it is your own views about yourself which are more important. ***Learn to see yourself with your own eyes and not from others' eyes.***

18. Don't fill your subconscious mind with all sorts of garbage

Your subconscious mind is a big store house for your conscious mind. Whatever you see, hear, think, feel and experience are all stored here as permanent memory. But, the problematic part is that, along with our thoughts and sense impressions, we are also throwing lot of emotional garbage and negativity (e.g. hatred, revenge, fear, anger, jealousy etc.) which is playing a real havoc here. Some people are constantly and mercilessly pouring negativity into their subconscious mind all the time even without being aware of it. Every time you think negative, it immediately gets fed into your subconscious mind. Whether you know about it or not, makes no difference in its effect.

Now the law is, whatever you have fed into your subconscious mind, it gives back the same to you. So all these negative impressions and emotions filled here, jump back and create ripples in conscious mind in the form of impulses, urges, and passions and keep it restless. ***The horrible dreams you see in the night are the result of this negative, careless and thoughtless programming of subconscious mind.***

Now what is the way out? You must begin immediately feeding the subconscious mind with strong and positive thoughts and emotions. This will gradually destroy negativities and impurities filled in the subconscious mind. Remember, ***Positive always overcomes negative***. For this, your conscious mind will have to be watchful and alert for each thought which it is thinking and should only allow positive thoughts to enter. To accomplish this, you will have to develop positive attitude towards everything, every event, every problem, every adversity and every misfortune by looking for hidden lessons and good in these things. This has been amply explained elsewhere.

Further, control your reactions and limit your attachments towards various worldly things and situations. The stronger your reactions and attachments towards a certain thing, the stronger are the impressions created in your subconscious mind and the stronger the impressions, the stronger is the turbulence generated in your conscious mind. ***In fact, it is our reactions and not the actions which are the root cause of our trouble.***

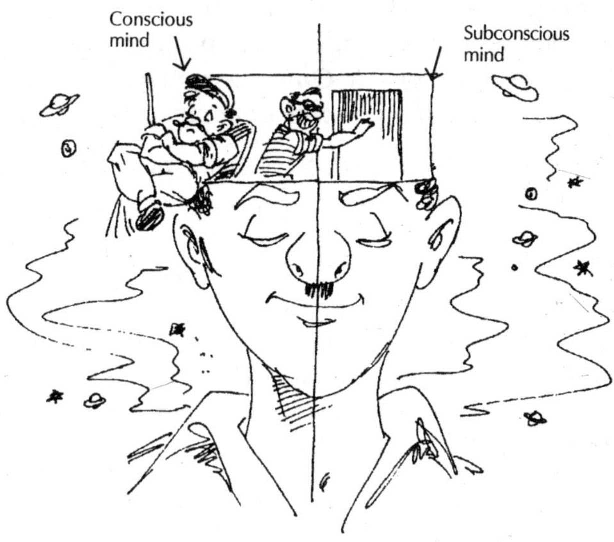

Conscious mind is like a watchman or a gatekeeper. Subconscious mind is like a store. If the watchman is sleeping, anything can enter in the store. But, if the watchman is alert, he may regulate the entry by allowing only desirable things and keeping out the undesirable ones.

19. Avoid making remarks/comments/ advice to others unless asked for

Concentrate only on your progress in life. Don't waste time in bothering and interfering in what others are doing. Also avoid making remarks, comments and finding faults about other's works because you are still not fit to do that. ***Only a person who has achieved perfection is fit to make a remark or comment upon others.***

Some people are in the habit of giving unnecessary advice to everyone whether asked for or not. Here also, you should give advice only when asked for and if you are not acquainted with the matter, apologize instead of giving wrong or vague advice. Similarly, ***any preaching which you want to give for the benefit of others, it is better to impart that from your behaviour rather than from words.*** Then it will have more weightage and force. Also remember that ***you can't mend any person against his own will.***

If you are in a managerial position where you have to get the work done from your subordinates, it is inevitable for you to make comments/remarks/advice about their works, but, again it should be made in the spirit of suggestion and no attitude of ego and domination should be involved.

20. Eliminate ego and doership feeling

In all the works or things you do, have the attitude that it is God's work and you are doing it under His guidance as a *sevak* or servant. He is the actual doer. You are simply a medium or an instrument in His hands. After completion of the work, again surrender it to God with reverence and humility. Never develop ego or *ahamkara* that it is you who could do this work and so you now expect admiration and reward for this. Because it is a fact of life that you, on your own, can't really do anything unless supported by God because of so many uncertainties associated with everything.

Also eliminate the ego of name, fame, property, wealth, family etc. because all these things are transient and will vanish some day. They have been given to you temporarily by the grace of God. *Ahamkara* or ego is a veil which doesn't allow you to come near to God. ***As soon as ego dissolves, you come face to face with*** **God.**

21. Always remain optimistic

No matter how many failures you have undergone in achieving a task, still remain optimistic about your success. ***Remember there is no force on earth or in heaven which can prevent you from achieving what you want to achieve provided you are determined for a right cause.*** The requirement is only a determined mind with firm faith in God.

Also remember that ***not even the slightest effort ever made by you goes in vain.*** This is the law of the nature. Various efforts, pains, discomforts borne by you now will definitely bring fruits later or sooner.

So even when things seem worst, don't quit and stick to the fight. You never know how close you are and you might succeed with another blow. The quotation: ***'In your failure lies the secret of your success'*** has been very thoughtfully written. ***Success/failure, pleasure/pain, night/day etc. are the two faces of the same coin and one can't be separated from the other. So where there is one, another is bound to be there as per natural laws.*** There is no need to be upset on account of this.

22. Learn to say 'No'

Be confident, straightforward, courageous and never hesitate to say 'No' when it is so demanded by situation. Your slight courage in saying 'No' can sometimes save you from unpleasantness of the whole life time. Don't get carried away by others' influence. ***Have your independent personality which should stand like a rock amidst even severe opposition if you are right.*** Also have the courage to raise your voice against any injustice or wrong being done. ***If you want to become great and unique, you will have to be different from the rest of the crowd.*** However, being straightforward shouldn't be confused with being arrogant. It is possible to be straightforward while still remaining polite and respectful. if possible, you can also explain the reasons to the other party for saying 'No'.

Some people say that by saying 'No' other person may feel annoyed and displeased, but, remember that your purpose in this life is not to please others. Your aim is self-development. Pleasure and displeasure of another person depends more of his own mentality rather than on what you say. For example, if a person is of negative mentality, he will view everything negatively no matter what you say or do. So instead of concentrating more on others, you should concentrate more on yourself as to what you are doing and whether it is right or wrong in your view.

23. Don't linger things

There are some people who have the habit of always postponing things. You ask them anything to do and they will always say 'tomorrow.' ***Successful people are those who get up from their seat and take immediate action. The right time for starting or doing an appropriate thing is just now and not tomorrow.***

No person has ever been able to do anything tomorrow. Whatever great things have happened in the world, they were done only by those persons who had always emphasized 'Today' and not 'Tomorrow.' Please note that 'tomorrow' never comes. What comes to you is always the 'present.'

Only talking and lingering things day by day is a sure sign of heading towards failure. So avoid laziness and take action 'here and now' and not in some imaginary future.

24. Always remain near to God

Whatever you intend to do, God should be in front of you. Feel His presence while talking, eating, walking, sleeping, travelling. Involve Him in all your activities. ***So long as you keep your hands in His hands, you are safe from all miseries of the world. As soon as your hand slips, you are surrounded by all sorts of fears, worries, anxieties, uncertainties, pains, discomforts, failures, disappointments.*** So make Him your partner in everything you do. Keeping your hands in His hands means that you remain connected to Him mentally. Gradually, as you nurture these feelings more and more, ***a stage will come when you will be so intensely connected with*** **God** ***that you will be knowing*** **God** ***and*** **God** ***only and you will be thinking, talking and doing everything in terms of*** **God.** This is a state of unimaginable joy and bliss. You will find it impossible to do anything without associating God. Everywhere you will find nothing, but, God. You will be so much intoxicated in His love.

Remain connected to God no matter what you are doing

25. There is nothing urgent or indispensable in the world

Some people remain under chronic time urgency or time pressure for completing various tasks. ***For them, if a work is not done within a specified time, either earth will fall down or the world will come to a halt.*** They also pass this stress to their subordinates by labelling everything 'very urgent' and also transfer their anxieties and restlessness to them.

Little do they realise that there is nothing called urgent or indispensable in this world. Anything can wait in this world for any length of time without any effect on the world. In fact, we are dependent on this world and not the world on us. World is self-supported and is being controlled by a much superior power. We needn't be sleepless about what will happen to the world without us. We are here to use this world and learn some lessons from it and not vice-versa.

Hence, perform various tasks from the point of view of your own learning and growth and there should be no feeling of panic or unrest for completing various works. Remember that even with all your panic, planning, arrangements, resources, expertise and precaution, there is no guarantee that you will achieve what you want to achieve. This is because of many uncertainties involved in the nature of world. *Our goal is to change and reform ourselves and not the world. Change in the world can happen by our own change, but, this (changing the world) is not our goal.*

Hence, just put in your sincere efforts and then leave everything to God.

26. There is nothing free of cost in this world

You have to pay a price for everything you get in this world. There is nothing called free under divine laws. ***Those things which apparently appear to come to you free like property of your ancestors, lotteries or even the bribe money, you***

repay it in some form or the other, though you can't directly see that. The conclusion from this is that never think of grabbing any property, money just out of way or by unfair means. It won't stay with you. It will drain away in some form or the other. Only whatever is due to you by virtue of your eligibility under Divine laws, will finally remain with you.

27. Enjoy the work, don't wait for the fruits

Learn to get pleasure right in the work itself which you are doing. ***As fruits are not in your hands and only in the hands of the Almighty, you should never depend upon the fruits for your pleasure.*** Suppose, you say you did hard work, still you did not get the fruits. Now why do you want to break your head in this analysis? This is God's business to analyse it. He may or may not give the fruits of your labour depending upon so many factors. ***You have done your duty and your part is over; now you go on to your next work. Why do you interfere in the part which God has to play?***

Note: For greater understanding of the principles of *Karma Yoga* in daily life, please refer to the article **'The Art of Relaxed & Efficient Working'** in my book **'How to Control Mind and be Stress-free'**.

28. Be flexible for adopting new changes and improvements

Change is the law of nature. The definition of the world is that which is subject to change. ***Every minute, changes are taking place. What we were one hour before, we are not now.***

Hence, don't oppose changes in life. Use changes as opportunities to learn and to grow further. This is the philosophy of the changes. If there are no changes, we will become static and dull. Resistance to change implies you are living in the state of inertia and inertia is a dead state. Science defines inertia as the tendency of a thing to give in the same state unless forced to change. ***Hence, learn to respect changes and apply them to your benefit instead of getting upset.***

Let us take an example of a change when you are transferred from one place to another. In this case, don't start all sorts of doubts/fears and negative thinking about your new place/new job. You will actually find that all these fears were only in your imagination. Actual things may be quite different there and you may also find some good things there compared to your previous place. In fact, if you want you can learn to grow even in negative circumstances. Your 'Will' can supercede the effect of all negativity and you can actually change a negative atmosphere into positive by your will-power, determination and positive thoughts.

Be also open to new ideas and suggestions. Don't lock the doors of your mind by keeping it rigidly fixed to some ideas, whims and fancies. Try and experiment new innovations, techniques and better ways to do a thing. ***Remember there is always a scope for further improvement, no matter at what stage you are.***

29. Avoid greediness, everything belongs to God

Don't claim anything as your own. Everything belongs to God. Whatever you claim your own, is actually given to you by God only for temporary use as means to achieve your ultimate goal, but, at some time or the other, all these possessions will leave you one by one as and when the purpose is served.

So never be attached to any worldly possession and don't identify yourself with them. ***You are simply a caretaker for some time.*** Hence, avoid greediness towards hoarding and collecting various worldly things which are perishable, changeable and subject to decay by their very nature. ***You should be able to leave any worldly possession at a moment's notice. Such should be your detachment towards worldly things.*** By this attitude you can eliminate jealousy also which is generated when you compare your possessions with others.

30. Small things are as important as big things

You should perform each and every task, however small it may be with one pointed and undivided attention. When everything starts appearing important to you, whether small or big, then you have actually started moving towards the path of greatness. ***Your successful completion of some big thing is not necessarily a sign of greatness.*** Even fools can sometimes do

heroic deeds, when outer circumstances are favourable. ***Your greatness is judged by how you perform each and every small thing in your life.*** For a truly great person both acts are done with the same dedication and absorption whether it is peeling off of a lemon or execution of a multi-crore project. This is also the principle of *karma-yoga* where all works are considered orders from the Divine and are done selflessly in a spirit of surrender to the Divine. ***There is no low or high work. There is no 'choice' or 'preference'.***

31. Don't show fickle mindedness in choosing or deciding something

In every field there is an endless variety in the world. A fickle-minded person becomes easily confused and mad in choosing and deciding anything, but, if you see deeply, there is an underlying unity in this great diversity. ***Diversity and duality, which we see in the world, are due to our ignorance.*** Actually the same thing is reflected in various forms. Only the outer coverings are different. The inside of everything is same. Spiritually realised persons are able to see this oneness in this endless variety and, therefore, are never disturbed and confused.

Because of this inherent oneness, you may choose anything or any field to work and you can find the same happiness from it as from any other thing, because ***it depends more on the consciousness with which you work rather than on the work itself.*** Hence, remain away from the rat race of comparison, which ultimately may end up in your becoming mad without any decision. Just choose an alternative (whether it be a job or selection of a bride or an article to be purchased from the market) for yourself after normal inspection and search, and then try to find satisfaction from that itself.

32. The more you give, the more you get

It is a wonderful divine law that ***whatever you give to others, comes back to you doubled or tripled whether it be knowledge or material things.*** Some people try to hide some knowledge and some material objects from others so that others may not reach to their level, but, the fact is that you gain more by giving. By giving your knowledge to others, you become more knowledgeable. By giving happiness to others, you become happier. By giving money to others, you become more prosperous. Hence, be liberal in giving to others. There is a maxim ***"whatever you give to others, you actually save it and whatever you keep with you, you actually lose it."***

Philosophy behind this magic of 'give' and 'take' is that whenever you give, your consciousness expands and you get closer to source of everything which is your real nature (or divine nature which is all bliss, happiness, peace and full of all goodness and virtues of life). On the other hand, whenever we think of only getting something from others, our consciousness contracts and we drift away from our real nature and get closer to our lower nature. This is a kind of selfish attitude which stops our growth and takes us further away from our ultimate goal.

It is the basic principle of life that any thing which is not used, exchanged, shared or whose flow is stopped, starts stagnating and anything which keeps on flowing remains fresh, alive and expanding. Further, you can be filled and replenished with anything new only when you empty yourself of the old.

33. Avoid selfishness and expand your consciousness

Leave the attitude of doing everything only for your own comforts, pleasure, profits. Remember the principle ***'the best way to keep yourself happy is to ensure that others are happy'.***

You should strive and work from the point of view that the whole world is going to be happy and better and not only yourself. Your effort should be directed like this. Let us illustrate it with an example. Suppose you don't have coolers in your office for summer season. One way is to think that 'I should have a cooler for my room so that at least I will be comfortable'. This is a selfish attitude. Another angle of thinking is that we should try to arrange coolers for the entire office so that all the persons are comfortable. This is a broader attitude by which the whole world will benefit.

By service and giving things to the needy, we expand our consciousness.

So your concern for well being shouldn't be confined only to you or your near and dear ones. It should encompass the whole world in it. If you see or hear someone suffering anywhere, it should bring in your heart same sympathy and concern as when you suffer yourself i.e. ***you should be able to look upon others' problems as your own by placing yourself mentally in their position***. You should have a clear realization that whatever comforts and luxuries we require, others also require and by whatever things we feel discomforts and pains, others also feel the same way by those things. When you actually start feeling in this way, then your consciousness has truly expanded to the concept of *Global* family. In this state, your relationship to everybody in the world is same. There is nobody near or far.

In short, you should always remember the maxim ***'In the well being and happiness of others lies your own happiness. If your neighbour is crying, you can't remain happy inspite of all luxuries'.***

34. Reduce unnecessary worldly involvements

World is like a big jungle. The more you enter into it, the more you are lost and confused. The way to your growth is not the quantitative accumulation of experiences in the world, but, it is the qualitative change in your consciousness. Many people wander mindlessly in this world running in one direction and then the other, seeking to have as many experiences as possible by changing many jobs, many homes, many lands, many relationships, many projects, etc. However, in the end these people are the most frustrated lot. Instead of running aimlessly towards various things of the world, focus on transformation of consciousness by changing your attitudes and by choosing few creative/constructive activities to work on.

Hence, involve in the worldly matters only to the extent required for your survival and carrying out your chosen professional duties. Avoid extra involvement, unnecessary roaming here & there, aimless mixing with lots of people, peeping and poking your nose here and there, meddling in others' affairs, etc. Similarly, reduce your worldly bondages by reducing number of investments, number of properties and assets, number of accounts and savings in your name, thus simplifying your life as much as possible. Unnecessary extra involvement in worldly affairs create distraction of mind and senses which is not conducive to your mental peace and spiritual development.

35. Have a good company

Be prudent in choosing your company as it has a great impact on you, though indirectly. Avoid mixing with people having negative attitudes and materialistic outlooks.

Have just a few friends whom you have properly tested over a period of time during various trials and who are in tune with your wavelength and once initiated, try to have enduring friendship with them. Frequent breaking of friendship is a sign of immature and undeveloped mind.

Great importance of 'Satsang' (association with the saints and the wise) in our scriptures is solely due to this fact that when you have a good virtuous and elevating company, we automatically change and improve effortlessly because of the constant impact of the positive vibrations and also by the law of induction according to which we always tend to imitate whatever we see, hear and observe.

36. Always keep a smile on your face

Try that while talking, walking, sitting, standing and at all times, you wear a natural smile on your face. ***This will ensure that you will naturally remain positive at all times effortlessly.*** It has been proved now that there is a great interrelationship between our gestures (Mudras) and emotions or moods. Both influence and are influenced by each other. That is to say if you change your gesture (may be deliberately), your emotions and moods are bound to change too. It is impossible to keep the same emotion which changing the gesture. Similarly if you are happy, it is impossible to keep your facial gesture wrinkled, frayed and tense. Your face is bound to be relaxed and pleasant to express the emotion of happiness.

By mentioning all this, I mean to say that ***by smiling, your body chemistry so changes that it is impossible to be stressed. Why not take advantage of this fact in making you light and free.*** Try and feel for yourself.

37. Reduce your expectations from others

Never expect anything from anybody. For example, you should not think that he is your son, so he should do this for you, he is your relative, so he should do that for you or you had done so much for that person, so he should at least do this much for you.

Please note that by helping someone, you are not doing any obligation to him. You are simply doing a Godly work and are basically helping yourself by elevating and purifying yourself by doing this good *karma*. The other person has simply given you an opportunity for doing so and you must be thankful for it.

As soon as the idea of getting something in return comes from a help extended, you have converted this pure act into a commercial bargain and the very ideal attached to your work has been lost. Moreover, any help done by us is actually being done by God. We have been chosen simply as a physical medium because of our wish to do so.

Hence, if someone doesn't reciprocate your help properly, don't have any ill-feeling or malice towards him, just be neutral. If someone reciprocates to your help, be grateful to him. Moreover, if at all we seek a reward for a good work or help, we should seek it from God and not from the person. ***Remember any good work ever done by us never goes in vain. It comes back to us suitably rewarded in some way or the other.***

38. Reduce collection of worldly things

Reduce your collection of worldly possessions and luxuries to the bare minimum which are just necessary for your survival and basic comforts. Normally it is observed that we collect much more than our requirements.

Tendency to hoard and collect more and more things whether you require them or not, eventually brings more and more anxieties, tensions and dissipation of your energy in ensuring their security, their regular maintenance and unnecessary blockage of space by them.

Unnecessary accumulation of things brings misery and tension

The reason of hoarding and collecting more and more things is that we start developing attachment and dependence on worldly things and luxuries forgetting that these are only temporary means for achieving something greater. No matter how much we are attached to them, they can't become a part of us. They are perishable and temporary by their very nature and are bound to leave us eventually. The more we become bound to them, the more disappointed and sad we will feel at their eventual loss. So before they start troubling you, it is better to leave their attachment on your own and become free. Try to have as little material possessions with you as are required for your basic comforts and survival and resist any temptation of unnecessary accumulations and additions.

39. Problems are an integral part of life

Most people think that when all their problems will be over, they will start their development plans of life. But, remember, ***problems are an integral part of life. They will never end. One problem will go, another will come.*** This is the nature of life. Life is designed like this that you will face various problems in life and learn the needed lessons to grow further. This is not only with you, it is with everybody. Nobody is without problems.

Hence, don't let problems interfere in the process of your development. In whatever miserable state you may be, go on developing yourself in whatever fronts you can. This is because whatever be your problems, some doors always remain open for you for further growth. ***All the doors are never closed for anybody, however wicked he may be.***

Also remember that ***there is no problem in the world which is greater than the strength of your mind and which can't be solved***. It is a general experience of life that when problems come to us in life, their solutions also come alongwith. ***We are never given to bear more than our capacity to bear.*** If we also open ourself to our Father (God) for guidance, a reasonable solution is found out much quicker for every problem.

It is very immature if somebody thinks or imagines that his life should be very comfortable and no problems should ever come to him. ***Take it for granted that there will always be ups and downs and unexpected things in life. You have to be prepared for anything in life.*** Such is the law. So, we should learn to live with problems gracefully. ***If we can learn to welcome problems, they will eventually lose their hold upon us and we will become their master instead of slave.***

You should also realise that compared to the comforts given to us by God, the problems are nothing. While enjoying comforts and luxuries of life, we are neither thanking God nor questioning why these luxuries have been given to us, but, in pains and problems, we become much perturbed. Is it not a fallacy? If we start doing the former, the hold of the latter will reduce. ***We should adopt thanks giving attitude to God even for the slightest comforts and luxuries provided to us.***

Note: For knowing the philosophy and Divine laws governing life's problems and limitations, please read article **'Problems and Limitations in Life'** in my book **'How to Control Mind and be Stress-free'.**

40. Give the world more than what you take from it

While living on earth, you are getting and have got so many things and benefits from your family, ancestors, society, country, world and from nature (air, water, sunshine and from the mother earth). ***Your life on earth would be considered worth only when you can give the world more than what you get from it.*** If you are being constantly fed from the society like a parasite

without contributing anything to the society, you are simply a burden on this earth. You can give something to the society in various ways by sharing your knowledge and experiences or doing some practical work based on your knowledge and experience which will lead to the betterment of the society and the world at large.

41. Be above limitations of life

You may have certain limitations in your life which are blocking your way to progress although you wish to progress. Please note that all these limitations are with you according to the law of *karma* or law of destiny. No one is to blame except yourself for your past *karmas*. ***So there is no point in cursing yourself or* God *or others.***

It is also true that many of these limitations can't be removed by you overnight i.e. you will have to live with them, ***but, remember, in whatever conditions/limitations you are, you can always make some changes. These changes will pave the way for bigger changes. All the doors are never closed for anyone. Everyone is given a chance to grow further and to come out of the vicious circle of law of* karma*, however bad a person may have been. No one is doomed to eternal hell.***

So, by your efforts, determination and applying the power of your free will, you can gradually frustrate the forces of your destiny and be above your destiny. ***Reaching at this stage, your destiny doesn't move you, but, you decide your destiny and the course of action of your life. By your efforts, will-power and determination, you can not only modify your destiny, but, even frustrate it fully.*** If you have a strong desire and will-power and are working for a right cause, there is no force on earth or in heaven which can prevent your success. All the forces of Universe will support your mission.

42. Regulate your diet for your mental well-being

Your diet has a considerable influence on your mind. The eatables like tea, coffee, alcohol, drugs, cigarette, cocoa, fried products, chillies, spices, sweets, too hot or too cold things, etc. have either stimulating or depressing effect on mind and disturb its equilibrium. Similarly overeating and eating something or the other at odd intervals is not conductive to good physical and mental health either. ***One of the secrets for good health***

is to always remain slightly hungry. Take plenty of water, vegetables and fruits for keeping your system clean and keeping your mind pure. Occasional fasting is very good for your health and for increasing the control of mind. Last but not the least, never take food in hurry or when tense. In this state of mind, food is not digested properly and it practically becomes poison. So, always eat with relaxed mind. If it is not possible, then skip the food.

Note: For more information on health related matters like diet, health parameters etc., please refer my books **'75 Health Charts'** and **'Foods that are Killing You'**.

43. Do regular exercises

Regular stretching and aerobic exercises release pockets of tensions and tightness in your muscles and thus lead to muscular relaxation. ***This physical relaxation in turn leads to mental relaxation because body and mind are closely interlinked.*** Aerobic exercises involving rapid movements also strengthen your lungs and heart and increase your general stamina and

power of resistance. Hence, make it a daily routine of performing physical exercises, jogging and *yogasanas*. Breathing exercises or *pranayama* are also beneficial in making your mind calm, serene and balanced.

Note: For knowledge and practice of various yogic and stretching exercises, readers may refer to my book **'Freedom from Cervical and Back Pain – The natural way.'**

44. Include rest and relaxation phases in your routine

Your daily activity must be balanced by proper intervals of relaxation. If this balance is disturbed, your efficiency goes down and inspite of increased working hours, you give less output. In relaxation, you have to relax your body and mind both. Physical relaxation is obtained by laying your body horizontally in *savasana* on the floor or firm bed after shaking and stretching each portion of body a little bit. Mental relaxation is obtained

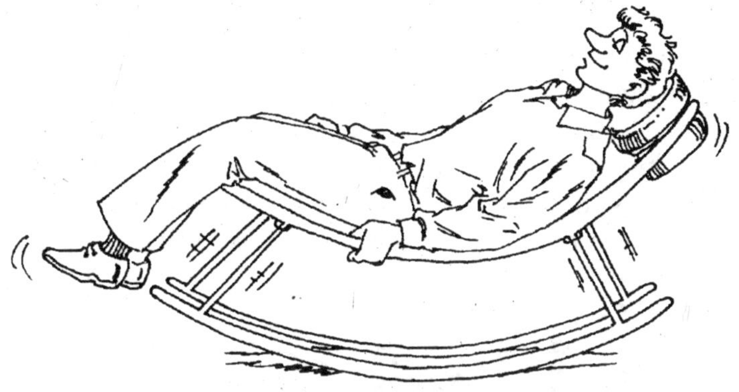

by focussing mind on a single object or stimulus e.g., on breathing or some *mantra* etc. This helps in stilling thousands of thoughts which flash through mind every minute. In true relaxation, you totally forget your body and surroundings.

By such conscious relaxation at frequent intervals between your activities, you recharge yourself with new energy to work.

Note: To have more knowledge of relaxation techniques please refer chapter on **'stress'** in my book **'How to Control Mind and be Stress-free'** and chapter on **'Relaxation Therapy'** in my book **'How to Overcome Fear'.**

45. Improve quality of your sleep

It is also very important how you go to sleep at night and the quality of your sleep. Just allowing the mind to go wild and wander aimlessly here and there before sleep, doesn't bring about a good quality of sleep. You get caught up in all sorts of ugly dreams in which you cry, shout, kick, jump, give and receive blows, wrestle and get up in the morning restless and tired instead of being charged with vitality and freshness. For good sleep, it is very important as to how you spend the last hour just before sleeping. It is a good idea to read a noble and mind-elevating book just before you go to sleep and also to fix your mind on some neutral thing (like breathing, recitation of some *mantra,* counting of numbers etc.) instead of allowing your mind to wander aimlessly. You can also do some self introspection before sleep and give necessary autosuggestions to improve yourself. Just before sleep, these suggestions are very easily caught and acted upon by your subconscious mind.

Irregular lifestyle and disturbed mind before going to sleep may lead to nightmares instead of sound and restful sleep.

The kind of life you lead also has a bearing on the quality of your sleep. For example, *Satwik* food and *Satwik* lifestyle bring good quality of sleep while *Rajasik* and *Tamsik* lifestyles lead to nightmares.

Your posture during sleep, thickness of pillow, thickness and type of mattress – all these things also matter in the quality of sleep. Even the direction in which you are sleeping also affects your sleep. For example, it is not recommended to sleep with your head on the northern side because it creates misalignment between your energy and the earth's magnetic energy.

46. Remain above diseases of the body

Body is a physical machine and is subject to all kinds of pains, aches and diseases depending upon how much you care for it and so many other factors.

In addition to various other physical means to alleviate the pain, we can also use mind power to eliminate pain because ***body is under direct control of mind. We can remove pain sensitivity by dissociating our mind from the body*** and focussing it upon some neutral thing e.g. on breathing, on some *mantra* or at some concrete object (as is done in some forms of meditation). We can also reduce pain by concentrating our mind inwardly (eyes closed) to the painful place and thereby increase the flow of *prana* there. This effect can be further enhanced by combining auto-suggestion and visualization of pain disappearance from the painful spot.

In the physical methods of alleviating pain, preference should be given to adopt nature cure methods for treatment. Nature cure treatments include hydrotherapy, *yoga*, fasting, mud therapy, massage, acupressure, heliotherapy, diet therapy, colour therapy, etc. Allopathic medicines should be taken to take care of serious and life-threatening situations only and not for permanent cure.

Note: To have greater understanding of **'Prana or life energy'** flowing in our body and its application in healing, please refer my book **'Healing Through Reiki'**.

For miscellaneous Yoga and Nature-cure treatments for alleviating diseases, please refer my books **'A layman's guide to Chronic Diseases'** and **'A layman's guide for Heart Care'**.

47. Eliminate the fear of death

Death is a very natural phenomenon of life and anything which is as per natural laws can neither be painful nor frightening except when we make it so by our faulty lifestyle and negative thinking. A great writer, 'Swift' has written –

"It is impossible that anything so natural, so necessary and so universal as death, should ever have been designed by Providence as an evil to mankind."

Death is just a transition from one life to another, a time for rest and self evaluation between two lives. ***After death you are just the same as before death except that you don't have a physical body and you reside in the Astral World with an astral body which is at different vibratory rate than the Physical World.*** Your mental attitudes and personality remain same after death. You don't become some superbeing or God after death.

Death can also be compared to sleep, the difference being that in ordinary sleep you wake in the same body while in death you wake up in the new body (Astral body).

Note: To understand more about the phenomenon of Death and removal of its fear, please refer my book, **'How to Overcome Fear'**.

48. Take initiative in setting things right

Most of the people simply go on accusing Government/people for various disorders, problems in the society, but they hardly do anything on their part to check these disorders. Simply accusing others won't help because there will always be some unscrupulous people who will be careless and corrupt in their duties. But once we take some initiative, by approaching them again and again for our problems, and write to them and their superiors off and on, some action will definitely emerge even if not to our full satisfaction.

Some people think why only they should take initiative for common problems of the masses. This is a narrow-minded approach that you will only bother for those things which directly benefit you. Expand your mind and consciousness to think of the benefit of everybody. After all, if the whole society benefits, you will also be benefitted indirectly.

So don't wait for others to start. If you find any disorder, lack of attention on the part of authorities in your surroundings, take initiative and contact appropriate authorities. It may involve some of your personal money and time, but seeing long term benefits, it is worthwhile taking the trouble. ***As an enlightened citizen, you must raise your voice against various disorders and injustice. It is your duty as well as right.***

49. Focus on changing yourself and not the world

World or society is made up of every single individual. Each person contributes to making the society or world as it is. Each person has a unique and important place in the world and leaves a definite impression or mark wherever he lives or works. World or society can't remain untouched by him.

Hence, if each person does his bit to change himself and his surroundings, it will be very easy to change the whole world. ***So, if we are keen to change the world, first thing is that I and you should start changing.*** Just accusing others or the society would not help to change the world.

It is an irresponsible statement, "Unless others change, changing myself alone won't help." Others may also follow your example after you start the process. ***Your change is definitely going to bring a change in the world, howsoever small it may be in proportion.*** Once you start changing, you will find that people around you and the environment around you automatically start changing by induction.

Only when you are happy, you can create happiness in the world around you.

But, remember that it is not your goal to change the world. Your goal is simply to change yourself. Change in the world will simply happen by your own change. There is no way to directly change the world. It is simply a happening and not a doing. *In other words, we can say that* ***the only contribution you can make in changing the world is to change yourself.***

50. Learn to forget and forgive

If someone does anything bad to you, your immediate reaction is to take revenge and do more harm to him. But spirituality teaches us to develop the attitude of forgiveness and not to take revenge, but ignore and forgive the ills of others. It is said that ***'revenge is such a game in which players die, but the game never ends'.*** Example of Jesus Christ is worth quoting here in this regard. He had requested God to forgive those who were responsible for his crucification.

Forgiveness acts as a soothing balm for your burning heart and makes you immediately light and free. It doesn't matter whether other person deserves forgiveness or not, but at least you deserve your peace of mind. The burden of hatred and malice which you carry with you by not forgiving someone, harms you much more than the person who has harmed you.

Jesus taught forgiveness.

Forgiveness means completely forgetting and burning the issue forever. If you say that you can forgive, but, you won't forget, it means you haven't forgiven and you have simply suppressed the matter beneath your conscious mind.

Forgiveness is mainly for releasing yourself from negative feelings and mental unrest. It doesn't mean that the person concerned has escaped the results of his wrong actions. There is a cosmic justice which doesn't spare anybody and takes care of everything. But you needn't break your head over it.

51. Avoid suspicions/doubts, have faith

Always keeping a suspicious/doubtful attitude about others is a negtive state of mind. ***Don't start with bias in your mind that other person is a cheat and will definitely deceive or loot you.*** There is a quote which says *"It is better to be deceived rather than mistrust a person"*.

Hence always start your interaction with faith and trust in others. Even then, if someone cheats you, he is actually cheating himself first. He suffers much more for this act according to the law of *karma* than the harm done by him to you. Any person doing good or bad to you will automatically enjoy or suffer according to the divine laws. Why do you bother about that? ***No person can ever escape from any evil deed done by him, irrespective of whether this evil deed has been done under the sea or above the sky.***

52. Be honest, truthful and righteous in your dealings

Remember this divine law: ***'Truth can never fall and untruth can never stand'.*** Temporarily you may be enamoured by the glamour of untruth and dishonesty, ***but, in the long run only truth prevails and wins. The boat of truth may shake amidst trials of life, but, it never drowns.***

Any bad actions done under the influence of untruth, dishonesty or cheating have their inevitable adverse reactions on the person from whom they originated. ***Results of our actions may be delayed, but, are never lost. There is an inevitable reward for good deeds and inescapable punishment for bad ones.***

Be same inside and outside i.e. ***your thoughts, words and deeds should show resemblance with each other. This is the true test of righteous person.*** But, normally it is seen nowadays that people have two faces. One is real and the other is artificial to show to others which is like a false mask worn by them. So their inside and outside don't match.

Truth can't be hidden. It has a force which doesn't rest until it is revealed. Any righteous action being done by you is also supported by God.

53. There are pros and cons in everything in the material world

Definition of the world is that which is dual in nature, meaning thereby that everything is made of two opposite aspects, e.g. day-night, life-death, summer-winter, male-female, young-old, pleasure-pain, excitement-sorrow and association-disassociation.

These two aspects can't be separated from each other. They are inbuilt in the nature of worldly things. They are the two faces of the same coin.

From this, it is concluded that anything which gives you pleasure must give pain too. Any person or thing which associates with you must also dissociate or leave you at some time. If you have got some gain or profit sometime, you will also suffer loss at some other time. If you have certain advantages from something, you will have certain disadvantages also. For example, when you marry, you have certain pleasures

and advantages, but, you have certain disadvantages too in the form of increased responsibilities. Similarly, you may have a house somewhere. You have certain advantages by it, but, certain anxieties and tensions are also associated with it. Same is the case with everything. ***Sometimes people see only one***

aspect of a thing and draw their conclusion that it is very good or bad. But, actually they forget to see the other aspect. This is why it is said that what appears is not always the reality.

The above mentioned law is also called the law of Divine Balance. So according to it, if you don't want pains and discomforts in your life, you will have to leave the desire for pleasures and luxuries also. ***If you don't want insult, you will have to leave the desire for praise also.***

Realizing this, reduce your indulgence in worldly pleasures and material desires. ***The best way to remain unaffected by this dual nature of the world is to deal with worldly things and incidents with a detached outlook as if you are merely a spectator i.e. neither get elated in success nor grieved in failure. Remain evenminded in gain/loss, success/failure, praise/insult.*** Once you reach to this mental level, you become free from the clutches of dualities.

Everlasting happiness or bliss which is free from any opposite aspect comes from inside, the deep recesses of your inner self (soul). This is what we should strive to get through meditation and other practices of yoga.

54. Depend only on God for help

For any help needed, depend solely on God. He only can provide real and lasting help. ***To make yourself eligible for this help, the only requirement is that you have to mentally feel yourself connected to God and have total faith in His benevolence and protection.*** God may choose any physical media to help you. You should see only inspiration of God in the help being provided by your relatives, neighbours or friends.

Always remember God

You should never feel yourself alone in the world. You have infinite power available with you of your own soul and of your father God – only waiting to be tapped.

55. Consider your children as the children of God

Your children are as much the children of God as you are. You and your children bear the same relationship to God. ***Your children are also directly answerable to God and not through you. You are simply caretakers of your children for a certain period. You are not the controller of their destiny.*** They have their independent destiny. With you their relationship is only temporary. You will leave the world after some time. Their lasting and permanent relationship is with God only who can provide them real protection. **God's *responsibility towards your children is much more than your responsibility towards them.***

With this knowledge in mind, you should rear up your children as God's servants, leaving unnecessary emotional ties and illusory attachment.

56. Choose appropriate colours

It has been proved now by Medical Science and nature cure practitioners that colours have a very profound effect on your body and mind. In fact, 'Colour therapy' has emerged as a separate healing technique both for body and mind. In this, the seven colours of sunlight (VIBGYOR) are used for healing. Each colour has a different effect on body and mind. For example, blue, violet and indigo colours give a cooling effect to mind. Green colour gives a balancing effect. Red, orange and yellow give stimulating effects to a dull mind and fill it with love, enthusiasm and vitality. White is a mixture of all these seven colours and is associated with purity and spirituality. This is the reason why it is frequently used in religious rituals and ceremonies. This is also the reason why it looks so pleasant to sit in sunlight which is a mixture of these seven colours.

Seven colours of sunlight have different rejuvenating effect on our body and mind.

Black colour is the absence of all colours and indicates hatred and malice. It makes mind dull, lazy and full of inertia. Dark brown and grey colours indicate selfishness. Hence, these colours shouldn't be used. In fact, darker shades of all the good colours (VIBGYOR) mentioned above should also be avoided because darkness indicates a transition towards black colour. Keeping this in mind, choose appropriate colours for your rooms, curtains, furniture, doors/windows and your clothes.

57. Maintain good postures

Your postures have a great effect on your mood and mental attitudes. Maintain good postures while standing, sitting, lying and walking. It helps to keep your body and mind active, bold and confident. Stooping, loose and slumping postures having unusual tilts and curvatures in your spines disturb the alignment of the body. This not only affects your body but also decreases the confidence of your mind and makes it dull and lazy because of the great interrelationship between the body and mind.

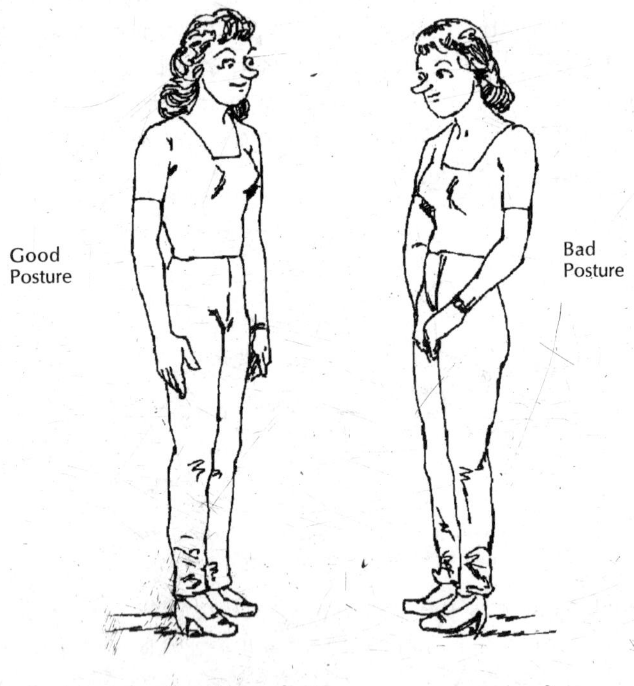

Note: For more details about good and bad postures, please refer my book, **'Freedom from Cervical and Back Pain'.**

58. Listen good, soothing music

Sound has a great impact on your mind. A distracted and restless mind can be easily centered by listening to good and melodious music and songs. Different effects of sound are due to their different types of vibrations. Every word or, in fact, every letter of a word which we utter, emits different kinds of vibrations in the atmosphere. Similarly the tone with which we utter a word also affects the quality of vibrations. Similarly different types of music which accompany the songs also leave different vibrations depending upon their quality.

Effect of music on mind and body is being explored with awful interest by modern science.

Seeing the effects of different types of sound and music on our body and mind, our yogic texts have classified various sounds into three categories:

(a) **Satwik sounds** – These sounds give inner joy and elevation to mind and calm down a distracted and tense mind. Devotional songs, bhajans, classical music, melodious songs of old movies, nature sounds (chirping of birds, moving breeze, waterfall, river water flowing, rainfall, tree leaves shaking etc.) come under this category.

(b) **Rajasik sounds** – These sounds stimulate and excite the mind and make it restless. Pop songs and most of the fast songs of the modern cinema come under this category.

(c) **Tamsik sounds** – These sounds make the mind dull and drowsy. You are well aware of such music and songs in which you just become bored, drowsy and sleepy.

Hence, cultivate the habit of listening good music to keep your mind elevated. Music is used nowadays as a part of therapy also.

59. Go close to nature whenever you find opportunity

Whenever you have any leisure, instead of wasting your time by loitering here and there and roaming in the supermarkets, go to some places where you are close to nature like gardens, forests, mountains, rivers, lakes, clouds, etc. Inhale fresh air there under open sky, listen to chirping of birds and sound of moving breeze. Take healing rays of sun on your body. It elevates and freshens up mind very much.

60. Maintain cleanliness and neatness in your surroundings

You might have heard this quote ***'Cleanliness is next to Godliness'. Cleanliness of your environment has a great effect on the state of your mind.***

Keep your work environment and house environment totally neat and clean. Don't let the dirt accumulate here and there. See that drainage and sewage system is perfect. There is no accumulation of water and chokage in system anywhere. Whenever you find any such flaw, show promptness in lodging complaint with the concerned authorities.

Don't let the things in your house or office be kept randomly here and there. Everything should go to its proper place instantly after its use. Everything should have a designated place for its storage.

External cleanliness of your body and clothes is similarly essential. Keeping your mouth, nose, eyes and face frequently clean after you eat something or come to your home from outside, are all efforts in the same direction.

Install air-fresheners in your house if necessary and use *agarbattis* to purify the air off and on.

61. Temperature, humidity, air pollution and noise affect your mind

There is an optimum level of temperature, humidity and sound at which your body and mind function best. For example, optimum value of temperature is 20-25°C, for humidity it is 45-50% (relative humidity), comfortable level of sound is 45 decibels. Variation from these optimum levels upsets the balance of body and mind and reduces their efficiency. Hence, one should try to spend most part of the day under these optimum levels of the above parameters.

Loud noise is as harmful to the body and mind as any other source of pollution.

Atmospheric pollution also has an adverse effect on your mind. Carbonmonoxide in polluted air reduces the ability of body to extract proper amount of oxygen. Deficiency of oxygen in blood affects brain functioning and, therefore, affects mind. Other chemicals in polluted air also have an adverse effect on body and mind.

62. Install good photos and pictures

What we see (visual stimulus) has great effect on our mind and affects our psyche positively or negatively according to its nature. If we install such pictures and photographs on the walls of our house and office which have an elevating effect on the mind, it is very useful to us. Photographs of enlightened and great men, pictures of natural sceneries, pictures of spiritual/religious places and temples/churches/mosques/gurudwaras etc. are very good in this regard. It may also be noted that effect of actual photographs is much more than handmade pictures because a photograph is said to possess the actual vibrational content of that person/ place. Such types of pictures as mentioned above come under 'Satwik' category.

On the other hand, Rajasik & Tamasik pictures are pretty harmful for mind. All the glamorous scenes we see in modern life, come under Rajasik category. Instead of calming the mind, they make it distracted and confused. Tamasik scenery, on the other hand, dulls the mind and makes it depressed and lethargic.

63. Go on disposing of rubbish regularly

Over a span of time, lot of old rubbish accumulates in our home and workplace which is no longer required by us. It is a constant tax on our energy to maintain it constantly without any output from it. We should cultivate the habit of regularly disposing of old waste materials to give place to new things. Either sell the old waste materials or donate it to the needy. It is not worth to have tension on account of the security and maintenance of old waste materials.

One very good technique for preventing your house from being junkyard is that whenever you buy a new thing, also dispose of some old thing. This formula of ***'one in and one out'*** will always help to keep your house neat and clean which, in turn, will keep you light and prevent your frayed eyebrows whenever you see junk in your house. Another alternative is to fix up a certain date of each month as 'Scrap disposal day', on which each member of family will search his own belongings, table drawers, room and surroundings and remove the unwanted scrap to a common place from where it can be disposed.

64. Add humour and laughter in your routine

Humour in your life has a great role in opening up the various psychological blockages in your mind. Your mind becomes open and fresh and comes out of its self created darkness by a full and hearty laughter. A good laughter completely decongests your brain and an increased amount of blood rushes there to nourish those ill fed areas. Hence, insert some humour and laughter deliberately in your routine.

Medical research has proved that during laughter body manufactures increased amount of 'endorphins' which are natural pain-killers of the body and have a morphine like effect. This is how laughter helps in healing also in addition to the psychological benefits like removal of depression, sadness, worry, nervousness, hopelessness. After a good laughter, you invariably feel light, open and fresh.

If you find it difficult to laugh naturally, then read jokes, watch comedy serials on T.V., watch movies having lot of comedies and fun, hear comic poetry, read comic stories. Maybe you can make a routine in your family that someone or the other will crack one joke daily while at the dinner table.

65. Don't be anxious to know your future

Some people waste lot of their time in consulting palmists, astrologers, numerologists etc. to know what exactly is in store for them in the future. In this connection, please note two points. First is that your destiny or future is not something which is very rigidly fixed. No fortune-teller can say with confidence that whatever he says will be hundred percent true. He can at best hint at various probabilities. This is because your future or destiny is alterable to some extent depending upon various factors. ***There have been people who are reported to have changed their destiny completely by their present efforts and reframed a completely new destiny for them. In other words, they took the control of their destiny in their own hands.***

Secondly, even if you believe in a predetermined future, what are you going to get by knowing it when you can't change it. You will simply make your life miserable and add unnecessary anxieties and tensions because ***it is sure that everything in future is not going to happen as you want. Some adverse things are inevitable in future not only for you, but, with everybody because life is like that, a mixture of pleasure and pain.*** In fact, by constant anxieties and fears about a certain thing to happen, we make it happen as self fulfilling prophecy by law of psychic attraction even if it was not otherwise destined to happen.

The correct approach in life is that you simply go on facing with a bold and positive mind whatever is coming in the journey of your life. You should affirm **God *has ordained everything for my good and with the help of* God *and the strength of my mind, I can overcome any obstacle in my path, no matter whatever it is.***

66. Control your desires and craving for sensual enjoyment

Material desires and sensual enjoyments have no limit. The more you enjoy, the more you crave for them. One desire satisfied gives rise to host of other desires and the chain becomes endless. Limit your desires to your basic requirements and comforts and thereafter don't run after luxuries and add desire after desire. ***The pleasures obtained by gratification of material desires and sensual enjoyment are shortlived and mixed with pain.*** They don't give a permanent satisfaction. Hence, we should put a tight rein on our unlimited desires and craving for sensual enjoyments. Our mind and senses when under the control of lower nature, always want to be tickled with momentary pleasures, thrills & excitements. We have to overcome these pressures of lower nature to awaken into our higher nature. We have not come to this world for enjoying these inferior pleasures. We are entitled to a much higher kind of joy which is more permanent and much more satisfying than these momentary pleasures. Proper knowledge of laws of life and their application in practical life gives us access to such treasure of infinite joy.

Here, it should be noted that when we say to curtail 'sensual pleasures', it refers to only *'Rajasik* and *Tamasik* sensual pleasures' and not the *'Satwik* sensual pleasures'. For example, when you are enjoying sunshine in cold winter days, it is also sensual pleasure, but, it is of *'Satwik'* type and is encouraged rather than discouraged.

Similarly, distinction between desires and needs is required to be well understood. Needs are related to your survival and basic comforts while the word 'Desire' in yoga is used for tendency to run after *Rajasik/Tamasik* sensual pleasures and ego based pleasures (name, fame, power, status). On the other hand, desire for your growth, desire for knowing the truths of life are good desires and are very much different from material desires which are referred to above.

Note: To know about the detailed philosophy behind **'Desires and Pleasures'** etc., please refer to **'mind elevating articles'** in my other book **'How to Control Mind and be Stress-free'**.

67. Don't indulge in the mad race for money

Nowadays, it is observed that people are indulging in a mad race of earning more and more money by whatever means. It becomes a sort of addiction for them that they simply have to go on increasing their money irrespective of whether they require it or not and then there is no end to this race. They become enmeshed in their own cage and are relieved only at their last breath, when a new race starts among the inheritors to capture the piled up property and money of the deceased. It can be seen here that the deceased spent more time in earning than in enjoying that money.

It is well said that after a limit the only use of money is to generate more money and increase your anxieties. If you want to be happy, remember this well tried and tested saying: ***'Money can give you everything except happiness'***.

Race for money takes you in a vicious circle ending nowhere.

68. Never give the excuse that you don't have time

This is a layman's excuse that 'I don't have time'. This is because when you are invited to attend a party in a five star hotel or when you are given free passes for a movie, you never say 'I don't have time.'

There is a quotation '***A busiest man has the greatest leisure***'. It means that even if a busiest man wants to do a thing, he can also do it by proper scheduling of his work. The only thing needed is your 'Desire and Will-power' to do a thing. If you don't have interest or desire, then even if you are free, you will not be able to do the thing. You will idle away your time in eating, sleeping, gossiping, watching T.V., cinema, reading stray novels and magazines, loitering in the market.

Hence, for executing your development plans or for doing some useful work for others/society, don't give the excuse of time. Rather make proper plans to incorporate them in your routine and start acting. ***We all have plenty of time if only we wish to do a thing.***

69. Live and work with the sole aim of your constant development

Whatever we do and wherever we are, ***our central aim in life should be to constantly grow physically, mentally and spiritually. Self-development is the only thing which is going to remain with us forever.*** All other things which are only means to this end are not important in the long run. They will all leave us on the way one by one.

Some people spend their lives as if somehow they are passing the time of their lives by doing whatever things. When there is nothing to do, these people get caught by boredom and time hangs heavy on them. They have no real growth of their personality.

While one's aim should be to grow constantly, but, at the same time, results of our efforts should be left on God. This way you will be free from the tyranny of pleasure, pain and boredom. You will always be filled with a unique divine joy and will grow stronger and stronger in developing your personality each and every moment.

Further, we can help others and society only when we ourselves are strong and developed in personality. ***If we ourselves are weak, what can we do for others?***

70. Don't waste anything

Develop the consciousness of not wasting anything. It is specially deplorable in our country where most people are not able to make their both ends meet. Apart from being harmful in respect of country's economy, tendency of wasting is a sign of undeveloped and narrow consciousness.

Wastage may be of eatables, paper, water, electricity, etc. If you see somewhere a water tap open, an electric light unnecessarily switched on, develop a consciousness to close them. Ignoring such things, thinking that it is nation's loss and not your own, reflects a narrow outlook. This type of feeling only brings you and your country down.

Similarly, if anything is lying wasted in your house and not of any use, donate it to somebody, who actually is in the need of it, rather than allowing it to be eaten by rust or insects.

71. Don't be fussy over trifles

Be broadminded. Don't make small matters a big issue. Develop forgetfulness and forgiveness. ***Being fussy over trifles only satisfies your false ego.*** It serves no useful purpose. Similarly, for taking decision of smaller matters, don't waste too much of your time. Rather, delegate these matters to your junior officers to enable their confidence to grow. ***Don't develop false ego that world is running only because of you. Realise that everybody is equally important in running the world*** and has also got the same potential as you have. You are not something unique.

72. Anger is a sign of weakness

Some people say that without anger it is not possible to get the work done. But, it is not so. ***You can get the work done from the force of your personality rather than from anger. Your saying something seriously should be enough to get the man moving. Your words and thought itself have a great power.*** Anger indirectly means that you are not able to accept or digest an unfavourable thing and you have grown mentally weaker. As a spiritual seeker, you must be able to face any situation or person in life with calm and even mind, no matter how bitter it may be. A person is likely to understand you more, if you explain a thing without anger, but, with firmness.

Note: For more details about physiology and psychology of anger, please read my book **'How to Control Anger'.**

73. You are not indispensable for the world

Please note that world is not going to stop or run because of you and me. It was going on when we were not here; it will go on when we will not be here. ***We are just a momentary existence here deriving some lessons and training from this great school of learning.*** World doesn't demand anything from us. It is self supporting. Only we are utilizing the world to grow and survive. By doing something great, you are basically helping yourself and not the world. ***Hence, avoid any anxieties, worries as to what will happen, if you are not there nor develop any pride that things are running only because of you.***

Similarly, you should also not have unnecessary anxieties and worries about bringing up of your family. They are also being fed and survived by Almighty God and not you. You are simply an instrument of God to bring them up working as a servant or caretaker or messenger under His guidance and utilizing this opportunity for your growth.

74. Don't advertise your problems/difficulties to others

Some people have the habit of always highlighting their problems and difficulties here and there and to anyone they meet. ***Except when you really need a help from someone, don't advertise your problems and difficulties to others.*** Keep them to yourself while at the same time making your efforts for the remedy.

By the very nature of a normal human psychology, nobody is interested in your problems. Everybody is interested only in his or her problems. By constantly listening to your problems, he will either feel bored or simply get a momentary pleasure and satisfaction at seeing your problems more than his. Moreover, at the first place itself it shows our narrow-mindedness and immaturity when we are all the time oozing out our problems to others because it indicates that we are taking worldly problems too seriously which actually are a very normal and passing phenomena of everybody's life. Of course, if you so desire, you can always take advice to solve your problem from a person who, you think, is more mature, knowledgeable and experienced than you in this field.

Similarly, ***avoid the habit of constant complaining and bickerings about various things***. This indicates an immature and weak mind. Also don't give excuses and clarifications to people about various things unless asked for. Let people think good or bad about you according to their mentality. It shouldn't matter to you much about what they think.

75. Develop tolerance

Tolerance is the highest virtue. ***Be strict for yourself, but, tolerant for the shortcomings and defects of others.***

Develop tolerance for the harms done by others to you, for the harsh words, insults and injuries inflicted by others on you. You should be able to easily forget and forgive the misdoings of others. This strengthens your mind. Gradually your mind becomes immune to all harmful effects directed against you. A tolerant person can achieve any height crossing all the barriers.

However, when somebody's activities appear harmful for the society or mankind at large, you must raise your voice as an enlightened person of the society and shouldn't remain silent. Tolerance and timidity are two different things. **Tolerance is a power while timidity is weakness.** Timidity is out of helplessness and compulsion but tolerance is out of right understanding.

But, raising voice doesn't mean anger, shouting, violence or destroying public property. You should raise your voice by actively reporting the matter both verbally and in writing to the appropriate authorities and higher authorities in the hierarchy if lower authorities don't respond. Also mobilize some more well-wishers with you and meet appropriate authorities in a group of 4-5 persons which always has more impact than meeting alone.

76. Don't fight over religions

Don't try to establish the superiority of your religion over others. All religions are good. They are all different paths or schools to take you to God. Similarly, all *Gurus* are great. They are all teachers to provide you necessary teaching and guidance to reach your ultimate goal. Hence, the ultimate purpose is the same. Only the paths and teachers are different. You can choose whatever is convenient to you, but maintain the same respect for all religions and *Gurus*. ***At the highest level, all saints and*** **Gurus** ***become equal. There remains no difference.***

Hence, there is no question of unnecessary comparison and establishing superiority of one over the other. To me, there is no irreligious person than one who fights over comparison of religions. ***To become fanatic in a particular religion or faith is like putting a barrier over your mind which can't see beyond a particular limit.*** Unless you broaden your mind in this respect, you can't hope to reach the ultimate goal, which is God. You will get stuck at a particular point in your journey and won't be able to go ahead.

77. Don't try to be a master of everything

Knowledge of worldly matters is unlimited. It is not practically possible to have a perfect knowledge of everything by any person. So, be an expert in one line and serve the world in that line. In other areas, you can simply possess general knowledge for the purpose of general dealing.

Our final aim is the 'Knowledge of Self', which will only liberate us from all sufferings and miseries. Worldly knowledge can't give you that final Freedom or Bliss which you are looking for. Worldly knowledge is only for our survival and for serving the world in some area, and so it becomes only a means to that final aim, but, remember it very clearly that attainment of more and more worldly knowledge is not our goal. Our goal is the knowledge of life as to who am I? What is life? Who is God? What is my aim in life? What is the purpose of this Universe? These answers will only give you that fulfilment and peace which you are looking for.

78. Take and give help freely

There should be no hesitation or reservation in asking for and giving help to others. It is everybody's birthright as divine children of God to take or give help freely to each other. However, if someone refuses to give help or someone doesn't recognise the help extended by you, there should be no malice in your heart.

By helping others, our consciousness is uplifted and purified. We should be grateful to the other person who has given us an opportunity to do this divine act. By giving anything to others, either material help or knowledge/guidance, you don't become short of anything. Rather, by divine law, ***'the more you give, the more comes back to you'***.

79. Enjoy each moment of life

Lead your life in such a manner that you are enjoying every moment of it. Some people lead the life with the attitude that now they will struggle hard and live in hardships so that they can enjoy later in life. This is an incorrect attitude. ***You should learn to enjoy amidst working and struggling also.*** Remember that ***sitting idle with all material comforts around is not enjoyment. You may, in fact, get highly bored in this situation.*** Sometimes due to bodily incapacities at later stages, you can't enjoy even material comforts available to you. It is already explained that the ***enjoyment is in the mind and not in the objects. You can have enjoyment without objects also.*** Hence, relish each activity and moment of life, howsoever trivial it may be and don't dream of enjoying life at some later date which may never come or you may face some other difficulty at that time which you can't imagine now.

80. You can learn from everybody in the world

You should not look down upon any person. ***There is nobody in the world who knows nothing and there is nobody in the world who knows everything. Everybody knows something which you don't know,*** no matter at what social status and profession a person may be. Hence, try to learn something from everybody.

To practise this in your day-to-day life, keep your mind open while interacting with anybody. Always be on the lookout for the unique talent, experience and the knowledge of the person with whom you are dealing and try to partake something from it. After going somewhere and meeting a person, always ask yourself whether I have learned something or I have wasted my visit.

Try to learn something from everybody

81. Don't do or accept anything which is less than the best

As a divine child of God, you are entitled to have everything which is best. There is no reason why you should live a life of miseries, limitations and bondages. These are all your own creations.

But, to entitle yourself for this great privilege, you also have a great responsibility on your shoulders that you also have to give the best to the world in every aspect you are concerned. Hence, never compromise in doing or accepting anything which is less than the best. To practise this, ***everyday try to do your job a little better than you did the previous day.***

Learn new techniques whenever you find an opportunity to do so. Everyday you should feel better and wiser than the previous day.

However, the word 'best' shouldn't be confused with the strain of perfection. The word 'best' here means 'as best as you can' or 'as best as is possible' under the existing limitations. Perfection is attributed only to God. For more clarification of this point, see item no. 100.

82. Observe courtesy and good mannerism

In our day-to-day dealings, we should observe good mannerism, adequate courtesy and rules of a good civilized society. For example:

(a) Use the words 'thank you' and 'please' generously.

(b) Stand up when greeting and receiving an elderly visitor.

(c) Return all things you borrow in time.

(d) Avoid sarcastic remarks.

(e) Keep secrets upto you. Resist temptation to leak them. Think twice before divulging a secret to your close friend.

(f) Remember people's names who remain around you.

(g) Respect privacy; knock before you enter a room.

(h) Resist temptation to interrupt people in the middle while speaking whether you agree or disagree with them. Listen fully and attentively, whether you know that thing already or not. Speak at your turn only.

(i) Learn to disagree without irritability.

(j) Be punctual and conduct meetings in time, regardless of who is missing.

(k) Resist telling people how something should be done, unless asked for.

(l) Keep your promises and words.

(m) Don't discuss business in streets.

(n) Praise in public, criticize in private.

(o) Never hesitate to use the phrases 'I am sorry' or 'I did a mistake' or 'I need help' or 'I don't know.'

(p) Learn to show cheerfulness even when you don't feel like this.

(q) Spend less time in worrying about who is right or wrong and more time in deciding what's right.

(r) Never tell anyone that he looks tired, depressed or diseased.

(s) Be grateful and obliged for any help done by anybody.

(t) Return the borrowed vehicle with petrol tank full.

(u) Don't discuss salaries.

(v) Arrive at the work early and stay beyond quitting time.

(w) Leave everything a little better than you found it.

(x) Reserve some time exclusively for your family members and show them with your words and actions that how much you love them and how much they mean to you.

(y) When tempted to criticize, hold your tongue.

(z) Hear both sides before judging.

All these seemingly little things elevate you and others considerably.

83. Don't think or speak ill about anybody

Thoughts are very potent weapons. Whenever you think or speak ill about any person, you not only harm that person, but, you are also temporarily charged with those negative vibrations and, therefore, you harm yourself. You are further punished by the law of *karma* for harming someone by thought. Therefore, don't indulge in it. Any person doing good or bad will enjoy or suffer accordingly. Why do you bother for that? But, of course, if the acts of a certain person are coming in the way of your

growth or they are harming the society at large, then certainly you have to take some action in the larger interest of the society, but, this you can do without keeping any ill-will or feelings of revenge against that person or rather with the feelings of good wishes for that person to improve himself. You may have to use some diplomacy and tactfulness in the process.

In fact, it is also said metamorphically that ***you can't see a fault in another person unless the same fault exists in you***. In other words, faults seen by you in others are images of your own shortcomings. This view is based on the philosophy that the ***outer world which we see is the reflection of our own mental state or our inner world. The world in itself is neither good nor bad.***

84. We are all connected to each other

We may apparently feel all human beings as separate from each other. But, the fact is that this separation is only physical. Mentally we are all connected to each other. That is why we sense each other's pleasures and pains. ***Each mind is connected with every other mind and all the minds, in turn, are connected with cosmic mind (God).*** So, there is a great interrelationship between everybody. ***No human is an iceland in himself. Everybody's activity makes a ripple in the whole universe howsoever infinitesimal it may be. In fact, each mind is in communion with the whole world.***

Realising this truth, reduce selfishness in various endeavaurs and try to work for the welfare and good of all. In other words, shift your emphasis from **'I'**, **'me'** & **'mine'** to **'we'**, **'us'** & **'ours'**. In the good of 'all' is hidden your own good also.

85. We can learn from every situation

Human life is so designed that we will face various types of situations in life and learn various lessons from them and grow. There is no dearth of situations and opportunities for us in life. ***Every occasion is an experience for us. No two situations are alike. Every moment is different from the other although we may not notice it.*** No human life-graph is a straight line that you will continue to have the same type of life day and night. There are curves in life. ***Our job is to extract as much benefit from every experience as we can.*** Every occasion, no matter how trivial or insignificant it may appear, provides us with an opportunity to learn something or the other, if we can keep our mind open for learning.

'Gurumayi' (spiritual successor of Swami Muktananda) says, ***'Treat every situation in life like the work of an art. Don't waste any situation.'***

86. Don't compare

Some people are in the habit of comparing everything with others and always remain frustrated. Such persons should realise that there is no end of comparison in this vast world. ***You may reach to any position, but, always there will be people who will be above you and always there will be people who will be below you. This is the nature of the world.*** Similarly, howsoever beautiful and costliest things you may purchase, but, still there will be things which will be better than these. If today they do not exist, tomorrow they will appear. So, don't involve yourself in this mad race. Try to derive satisfaction from whatever little you have got and always keep this maxim in mind: ***'In this changeable world, there will always be a thing which will be better than the thing you can ever have.'***

'Comparison has no end'

87. Be independent, take your own decisions

Some people have the habit of looking towards others for taking any decisions for themselves. This is indicative of a weak mind lacking self confidence. ***You should try at most of the times to solve your problems by yourself and take your own decisions.*** You may consult others, but, the final decision about yourself has to be yours. People depending upon others for running their lives are never a success. ***People who have become great and successful are so because they have taken some risks and independent decisions in their life.*** It is said that, ***'To become great you have to cross one ditch or the other in your life'.***

Have trust in yourself

88. Learn to appreciate others

Learn to appreciate others for the good things and good works done by them. This encourages them and results in a healthy atmosphere around. Seeing good in others will always keep you mentally positive and cheerful. ***No matter how bad a person is, but, every person has some 'good' in him.***

If you are at a managerial position somewhere, compliment your employees even for small improvements and never lose an opportunity to tell the good employees how much they mean to the company.

89. Be humble as you rise more and more

There is a maxim that ***'Greatest man is he who is the servant of all'***. Great persons become more and more humble as they gain more and more wealth, power, status and honour. Becoming proud on getting name, fame, money and power is a sign of undeveloped mind. You should make no attempt to show off any of your material status namely name, fame, wealth, power to others. Simply submit them to God. All these things belong to God and not to you. ***Pride and arrogance lead to a definite downfall of the person. This is a divine law and doesn't spare anyone.***

At whatever level in the society you may be sitting, you should still remain as much accessible to the lowest as to the highest. You should realise that distinctions of levels in office or society are for the sake of performance or organisation of work and not for dominating others. ***As children of God we all are equal. Moreover the real sense of highness comes from the qualities and virtues you have and not from powers, wealth or official status.*** It is said that you are fit for a position only if you totally leave the idea of occupying that position. You might have heard the maxim ***'He is fit to rule who reluctantly wears the crown'.*** Hence, erase even the slightest feeling of egotism and superiority of your position. ***Work as a servant of God and on God's behalf.***

90. Be grateful to God for every joy and comfort of your life

In this life, we are enjoying many comforts. Most of us are fortunate in having all our basic needs duly fulfilled. For example, we have got a house to live in, clothes to wear, water to drink, family to share our joys and sorrows, neighbours to fulfil our social needs, a job for earning livelihood and keep us busy and good health to carry out our activities for 70-80 years.

But, have we ever pondered as to by whose grace are we enjoying all these? Was it within our power or for that matter, within the power of any of the human beings on the earth to provide such large life-sustaining infrastructure for us? Certainly not. All this miraculous set up for our comfortable living can only be created and sustained by the Almighty God. So then, is it not our sacred duty to thank and be grateful to God while availing His grace?

In fact, it is a sin to enjoy any benefit without ever bothering as to who is the source of these enjoyments. Just going on enjoying comforts of life without ever stopping to think of the merciful God is highly selfish on our part as a human being. One should constantly be grateful to God for the slightest comfort and luxury one is enjoying or availing in his life.

Going one step further, one should also be thankful to the person who has become God's *'Nimmit'* or agent in providing help to you or fulfilling your need. The very fact that he has agreed to become God's *'Nimmit'* is enough to thank him.

91. Don't always misunderstand others

There are some people who always misunderstand others. They always feel that the activities of other persons are aimed at harming and insulting them. Any piece of suggestion and comment on their work is taken by them as a personal insult and criticism. Every conversation is taken by them as a challenge to debate.

In fact, it is one of basic instincts of our lower nature to perceive every unknown or new thing as a threat to us. Maharishi Patanjali in his *Yogasutras* also says, ***Nature of mind is to doubt***. But, by proper contemplation and right knowledge, this natural weakness is to be overcome and sublimated. If we ponder over deeply, we will realise that ***this feeling of misunderstanding develops because of the feeling of separation from others.*** We feel that we are separate from the remaining world and, therefore, the whole world appears to us as our enemy with whom we will have to wage a constant war to ensure our survival. But, is it so? The fact is that we are not separate from one another. We all are connected and are an integral part of this overall creation. Our needs and goals are common. The points on which we differ with others are less while the points on which we agree are more. So, where is the scope for misunderstanding?

Hence, in your interaction with others, don't start with this notion that the other person is your enemy and wants to harm you. Rather, you should start from the notion that the other person is good. Only when he proves himself to be bad by his acts, then only you should change your opinion.

92. Let power come to you on its own

Many people, although having sufficient potential, don't start anything worthwhile in life because they complain that they don't have necessary powers, resources and facilities for doing such things.

In this connection, please remember that for achieving anything great, nobody will come to you with folded hands saying 'Sir, these are the things you will need for becoming great. So, kindly accept them.' In fact, the process is reverse. As you show or prove your greatness, the necessary things will automatically be drawn towards you by a mysterious divine process. There is a saying, ***'You do the thing and you will have the power'.***

So, the correct approach is that if you really want to do any great thing, start the project with whatever little resources, powers and knowledge you are having. You will notice that as you proceed, other necessary things will automatically be drawn towards you gradually as per your needs. It is rightly said that ***'Greatness is always earned by self efforts. It is seldom given as a gift to someone.'***

This is also a divine law that the more you run towards power, name, fame, status, the more they will run away from you. The more you are reluctant towards them, the more they will run towards you requesting you to accept them.

93. External circumstances can't create stress on their own

Some people have the wrong notion that some external factors or someone external of them is responsible for their stress and unless these external situations change, they can't be happy. But, this is an incorrect reasoning about the laws of stress causation. Often the people and situations around you can't be changed, but, it doesn't mean that you will remain stressed throughout the life. As mentioned earlier, ***it is not the external situations, but, your reactions towards them which cause the stress. You may control your reactions such that you are never affected emotionally, no matter what happens in the outside world.*** It is like insulating your mind from the impact of external situations or making your mind independent of external circumstances. In these situations, the mind behaves as the master and the external circumstances as its servants so that mind controls the external circumstances instead of being controlled by them.

External circumstances only provide the necessary material or fuel for causing stress. But, they themselves can't cause stress. Stress is caused only when this fuel is ignited by the negativities of mind. Hence, the primary cause of stress is in the mind. External conditions act only as a secondary cause. ***Without the support of mind, no condition or circumstance can act as a stressor.*** However, it doesn't mean that one shouldn't try to change his external environment or circumstances to the better. To whatever extent you can change your environment towards the better, you must do it. A positive environment is definitely a supporting factor in stress prevention.

Note: For more scientific understanding about Stress and Stressors, please refer my book **'How to Control Mind and be Stress-free'.**

94. Don't make catastrophe out of unpleasant events of life

In our life, many sad events may take place, but, they can't upset us unless we make catastrophe out of them by saying to ourselves that it is a life and death situation or the world is going to end or the earth is going to fall or any other similar catastrophic statements.

But, is it so? Is anything in life really so terrible? ***Experience of thousands of enlightened men who themselves faced many storms of life shows that there is nothing in this life which can be called catastrophic or unbearable. Everything can be accepted and handled with serenity.*** Showing reasonable concern over a sad event and taking remedial measures is quite alright, but, it is the overconcern and overanxiety which creates problem.

It is only when we start taking things unduly serious and giving them more weightage than they deserve that they start dominating us. Give only that much importance to a thing which it deserves. ***If you can learn to view the things from a distance***

This person is making catastrophe of the shortage of salt in the food.

with a larger perspective, you will find things are not as terrible as you imagined them from a narrow perspective. So, next time when you get disturbed in life by something, just ask yourself: ***'If this thing is really that important or serious so as to make you so much disturbed. Is it the most important thing in your life? What is the value of this thing compared to the ultimate goal of life? What is the worst that can happen to you in this situation?'*** You will find that this very questioning and challenging will unload your mind from the unwanted agony.

As mentioned earlier, taking things seriously and emotionally also builds strong impressions in our subconscious mind. These impressions then make us more susceptible to tension in future in the face of similar situations. Hence, you should try to face every situation in life without much emotional involvement in it so that no *samskaras* or impressions are formed in subconscious mind.

95. Learn to give up and let go

Some people think that the way to one's development and happiness is to accumulate as many things as possible, encounter as many people and relationships in life as possible, change as many jobs as possible, travel as many places as possible, etc.

But, unfortunately, when these very people look back upon their life at the fag end, they wonder what was it all about. Why did they do all this running about?

In fact, the truth is that happiness consists not in accumulating things, but, rather in giving up and letting go. The more you let go, the more relieved and relaxed you become. When you let go of everything, you become totally free. This letting go does not mean throwing and leaving everything you have. You may have everything, but, still you may be mentally detached from them. This is what is true letting go. This attitude is applied not only in the case of material possessions and experiences, but, also in respect of various emotions rooted in your mind. For example, suppose you have some anxieties in respect of a certain thing in your mind, some jealousy and hatred towards a certain person; just allow these feelings to drop like a stone falling in water and allow yourself to be free.

There is a tense discomfort in clinging to something while there is a feeling of relief and relaxation in giving up the thing. ***When you get attached or stuck towards a certain thing, freedom of your thought and action is lost*** and you are likely to think and act in the world in terms of those attachments. Thereby, you won't be able to see reality as it is and this ignorance of reality creates discomfort and disharmony.

96. Do you feel lonely and bored?

In spiritual parlance, a lonely person is he who does not know himself and who can't face himself and only such a person runs after other objects and persons to keep his mind occupied. When he doesn't have any object or person to engage his mind, he feels bored. **Boredom comes from wanting to have something but not having it. He doesn't realise that joy can be experienced without objects also by turning the attention within.** He fails to experience the internal joy and peace which is there with everybody in the deep recesses of one's soul or self.

But, to depend on other persons and objects for your gratification is highly illusory because nothing is going to remain permanently with you in this world. Everything will leave you one day and then either by choice or by force you will have to live only with yourself. Even in our normal day-to-day busy life, moments come when we are alone and are only with ourselves.

If you can't live alone, it means you are not at peace with yourself. There are many conflicts and disturbances inside you which start troubling you as soon as you sit alone. So, to avoid that you always want some external props in the form of objects and persons so that your mind may remain engrossed in outward things instead your internal disturbances. But, this is running away and diverting yourself from the real problems. These stopgap arrangements won't give you the eternal peace and satisfaction which you are craving for at the bottom of your heart. They are like 'Labyrinth' (*bhoolbhulaiya*).

Sooner or later you will have to come to terms with yourself for getting the peace you are craving for. ***Running away from yourself is never the way to attain peace.*** It only delays the attainment of peace. So, the crux of the matter is that you have to learn to like yourself, to live with yourself. If there are any disturbing factors in your personality, try to resolve them rather than running away from them. Remember that finally it is your own-self only which will live with you and not anything else in the world. At an advanced stage, you should develop an attitude such that you may feel alone even while in the crowd and feel in the midst of people even while living alone.

We have all made it a habit to stay in a crowd. We are afraid of being alone, even though the reality is that our aloneless is our truth. ***We come into the world alone, we are alone and alone we will depart.*** Is it not true that a person is always alone, even when surrounded by hundreds or thousands? ***Recognize your aloneness, know it and experience it. Everyday for a short time, live as though you are alone in the world. At this time, you are neither a husband nor a wife, neither a father nor a son, neither a teacher nor a student, neither a man nor a woman.*** You are just you.

97. Don't get upset over rejection and disapproval

Some people get very upset when they or their works or their opinions are rejected and disapproved by somebody. They start feeling that they are worthless and inferior compared to other people and consequently develop depression and hopelessness.

If you do so, you are making a very false assumption that the person rejecting you is always right and you are always wrong. But, the fact is that it is not always true. ***The person rejecting you may not be technically fit for evaluating you or he may be a biased and jealous person against you. So how can you take his evaluation to be correct?***

You should take the comments of the other person about you simply as a matter of his own opinion. You certainly needn't get upset over every difference of your opinion with others. In fact, when a person gives any opinion about you or your works, it tells more about the taste and mental state of that person rather than yours.

Instead of getting carried away by the opinions and judgements of others, you should, at such occasion, stop for a while and evaluate yourself against those opinions. If you feel that there is certainly a scope for improvement on that account, then take corrective measures. If you feel that there is no weight in the comments of other persons, just ignore them instead of giving them more weightage by constant thinking.

98. Eliminate self-centredness in your talking and dealings

There are some people whose whole conversation is filled with 'Me', 'Mine', 'I', e.g. 'I had done this', 'I like this', 'I only can do it', and so on. It appears from their talks that they constitute the whole world and there is nothing else in the world except them.

In fact, talking and thinking only of ourselves is a sign of very narrow and low level of consciousness by which we make ourselves very small. We no longer remain a part of this universe and a participant in great *'leela'* of God. We become separated and, therefore, feel discomfort and disharmony with the rest of the universe.

Consider yourself a part of this universe and part of grand *leela* of God which is unfolding here. ***You are not different from other persons. All of us have common needs and***

common goals. All of us bear the same relationship with God. Thinking and doing various works from the consideration of common benefit and from a universal vision is a sign of expanded consciousness and it truly fulfills our mission and goal on this earth. Doing everything from the viewpoint of only personal gain is highly selfish and unbecoming of us as human beings. This negates the very purpose of our existence in this world. Exercise your will-power to stop yourself whenever you are tempted to boast about yourself or to talk only about your own interests or problems. In fact, ***when consciousness is enlarged, the idea of living and working only for oneself appears quite absurd.***

99. Don't lower down your level to the level of the person who is misbehaving with you

In this life several moments come when other people start fighting and misbehaving with you for no valid reason, but, just out of their lower nature and wrong habit patterns. Automatic response of the innocent party in this situation is to fight back and retaliate to prove that it is the first party's fault who started the fight for nothing. But, the first party being governed by its lower or sub-human nature becomes more adamant and aggressive after listening such remarks. So, the matter escalates instead of diffusing.

So, what is the correct course of response in this matter? In such situations, you must realise that the person misbehaving with you is doing so because he is a slave of his lower nature. For his bad nature and lower state of mind, why should you get upset? Let him remain tense and upset because of his bad nature and temperament. You are not responsible for his state of mind.

By starting a fight with that person, you also lower down your level to his level which is not desirable. You should maintain your mental level and standard. The best course in such incidents is to ignore such a fellow. By bothering about him more and arguing with him about wrong or right, you are unnecessarily giving him more importance and weightage, which actually he doesn't deserve. If the person had necessary *'buddhi'* to appreciate your arguments, he wouldn't have started the illogical fight at the first place. It is like this that if you start explaining the logic of right and wrong to an animal; will it be of any use? So, the best course in such situations is to ignore, forget and not give any further energy to the opponent to prolong the fight. ***In fact, before starting any discussion or arguments with any person, you must think whether spending so much time & energy with this person is really of any use or you are just satisfying your false ego.*** Is this fellow or are his utterances really so important? Convince yourself by your higher mind (intellect) the futility of such confrontation.

You also know this thing clearly that for any right or wrong things done by any person, he will enjoy or suffer automatically through Divine justice. Nobody is spared on this account. So, it is not necessary for you to spend your lifetime in teaching lessons to everybody. Your approach should be to somehow find your way through all sorts of persons so that your growth and your works are not hampered.

100. Avoid strain of perfectionism and idealism

There are many people in the world, who remain under strain because they expect perfectionism in everything and they are not able to get it.

"I want perfect work from all my employees but I am not getting it."

In this connection, please understand that perfection is only attributed to 'God'. ***We human beings, by our very definition, are imperfect. No matter at what level we reach, we can't avoid making mistakes.*** We can reduce our imperfections by constant knowledge and practice, but, we can't achieve blotless perfection (A human being achieves perfection only when he attains the highest state of consciousness which is called *'moksha'* or *'nirvana'* or *'mukti'* or 'state of God Realisation'. At this stage, he doesn't remain an ordinary human being and becomes the copartner of God. He needn't further return to this earth for learning more lessons or attaining more perfection and is freed from the cycle of birth and death.)

There are some persons who insist on getting one single perfect solution of a problem. What is needed is that instead of stressing upon one single perfect solution of any problem, one should strive to get an adequate number of good solutions which, for our practical purposes, will be good enough to execute. ***Expecting only perfectionism and idealism in every situation will constantly lead to stress. We human beings are bound to make mistakes, no matter whatever we try.*** However, the aim should be to learn from these mistakes and reduce constantly our degree of imperfection as much as possible.

Committing mistakes is quite natural for human beings. There is nothing unusual or criminal in it. There is no need to hide yourself or feel ashamed of after committing mistakes. The important thing is to learn the necessary lessons from the mistakes and constantly improve yourself from A to B, B to C, C to D and so on. Don't remain stuck in your life's journey at one point. You have to improve, improve and improve every moment and in every sphere of your life. ***If we don't learn from our mistakes, we lose the benefit of the lesson which every mistake brings with it.***

101. Learn to adjust and compromise

Everyone has the desire that things in the life should go as he wishes and that the world should be kind and fair to him; that people should be respectful and polite to him and that only his views and ideas should be accepted and implemented.

Unfortunately, this is not so and it can never be so. This world is very complex and it has not been designed to cater only to your and my whims and needs. The world is running according to a certain scheme and divine laws and not according to my and your wishes and requirements.

There are certain things and forces acting on our lives over which we have no control. We should accept and respect these limitations. ***Instead of fighting with such things which we can't control and change, we should learn to adjust and compromise.*** Some people have a wrong notion that adjustment and compromise is a sign of weakness, slavery or surrender before another person. But, actually it is not so. ***You require much greater will-power and strength in adjusting with a person rather than fighting. Getting into confrontation with another person needs no will-power. Anybody can do this.***

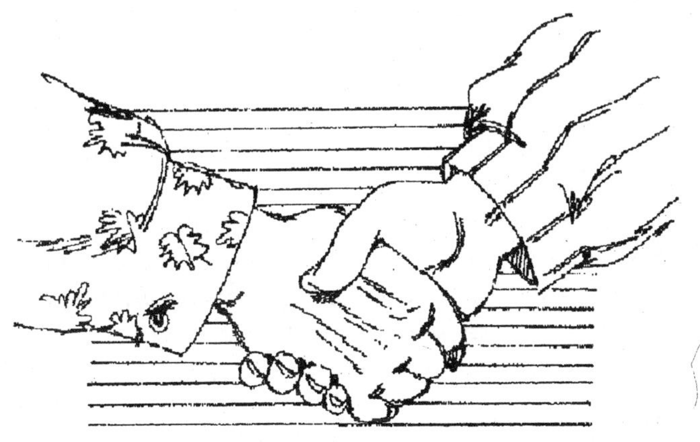

102. Avoid the strain of impressing others

This is one of the greatest sources of stress for a man in modern society that he wants to remain high in the opinion of others whether actually he is so or not. We can't stand rejection from the other people. Fear of other's opinion is the greatest threat that modern man has created for himself. ***We fail to recognize the tremendous strain we are putting on ourselves to live upto some kind of image in other's eyes.***

By trying to impress others and thereby getting joy, you are indirectly giving the key of your happiness to others. That is, if they want, they will make you happy and if they want they will make your life miserable. You simply become a puppet in the hands of others who will make you dance to their tune. In other words, you reduce yourself to a slave or beggar by mortgaging your happiness on the mercy of others.

Your happiness and contentment should rest in yourself and not in somebody's hands. You should do any work primarily from the point of view of your own satisfaction. You should derive the joy right from what you are doing. ***Your joy shouldn't wait for the time when somebody will come and appreciate your work.***

Don't give overweightage to other people's views about you as to whether they know your calibre or capabilities or whether they overestimate or underestimate you. There are many people in the world who don't know at all about you. Is it making any difference to you? ***Your estimation in your own eyes is much important. Other people's comments should be taken only objectively as an opportunity to reexamine yourself and take any corrective action, if required.*** Even if you find that you are weak in a certain area, it shouldn't cause much concern. In this diverse world, differences in the calibre of people are bound to be there. There is nothing unusual in it. In some areas, you may be better and in some areas, others may be better. To have a desire that you should be at the top in the world in all the areas and only you should be appreciated most in the world is highly illusory.

103. Learn to change your thoughts quickly and consciously

The mood you are having now is depending upon the thoughts which are there at present in your mind. If you change these thoughts and start thinking something else, surely your mood will change.

Now you have got a simple formula. Whenever you are feeling disturbed, just put your mind and thoughts on something pleasant. Immediately that disturbance will go. For example, suppose you are feeling worried about your son's health living in a hostel. Now you just divert your thoughts towards the urgent works you have to finish tomorrow in your office or the various meetings and appointments you have in your office tomorrow. Immediately those thoughts of worry have to go because mind can't think about many things at a time. It is, therefore, impossible to be disturbed by something unless you start thinking about that.

You can divert your mind towards some pleasant and entertaining thing. For example, you may start listening to some good music and melodious songs; you can take a mind elevating and spiritual book and can get absorbed in it. You can also watch a good T.V. serial or you can just go out in the open air and have a stroll in the nearby garden, forest or lake or you can also have a chit-chat with a good friend, if there is any nearby.

104. Continue to progress even in tragedies and misfortunes

There are some people who make their life completely dead and dull when any tragedy or misfortune strikes them. They move about depressingly and helplessly as if there is nothing in life. Till the emotional impact of tragedy wears out from their mind, they continue to spend life in this miserable state and, therefore, much useful time of their life goes waste.

Here again you should accept this fact that tragedies and misfortunes are part of everybody's life. ***Whether you like them or not, they will continue to come as per your destiny and the overall design of your life determined by the Almighty.*** There is nothing unusual and extraordinary in their falling on our head from time to time. Hence, instead of getting shocked by them, let us learn to accept, face and respect them. Many people refuse to accept that such and such thing should have happened to them and thereby they continue to remain stressed and mentally sick.

The sooner you learn to accept and then reconcile with the impending calamity, the sooner you will be at peace with yourself. You should learn to adjust with the impending disaster as quickly as possible and then start acting again with the same speed. ***The only reality in the world is change. How can you stop that? Life is like a river. It has to flow continuously. It can't be stopped at one particular point of life.*** Hence, remember this formula of 'accept, adjust and start acting again'.

105. Reduce expectations from your spouse

Your spouse is also like any other human being having all the weaknesses and strengths found in an ordinary person. Don't expect a flawless behaviour from him/her considering him/her a special and ideal human being. Doing so will be like living in a dream world. Like any other human being, she/he will also do many stupid things and display funny habits. In fact, you should expect such things in advance. Your ability lies in getting the best out of her/him by using whatever good qualities and abilities she/he has possessed. At the same time, you should learn to compromise/tolerate/adjust or even ignore bad qualities and irritants in his/her character. This is nothing unusual. Everybody has got some funny and peculiar characteristics which makes him/her different from others. In fact, your ability lies in preventing those circumstances which awaken the irritants in your spouse.

If you want to change any bad habit or disturbing behaviour of your spouse, it can never be done by preaching or scolding or criticizing. It can only be done by changing and adjusting yourself and not by trying to change your spouse. ***Remember that unless a person himself wants to change, nobody can change him. It is only by changing your own behaviour that you can expect another to make some changes in his/her behaviour. But, confrontation, argument, criticism has never been the way to change a person.*** Rather, it is observed that by this way the old habits and negative traits react more powerfully.

Further, you shouldn't have very high expectations and demands from your spouse. None of you is slave or servant of another. Both are supposed to support each other to grow. Both share equal responsibilities for maintaining stability and joy in relationship. ***Weaknesses of one are to be overcome or compensated by the qualities of the other.*** This is the ideal attitude that should be attached with this important relationship.

But, this is possible only by cooperation, compromise, tolerance, adjustment and respect for each other. However, if one of the spouses is not understanding and compromising, you should still continue to play your part in the desired and expected line, without showing any sign of frustration and depression. Consider it as a part of your destiny. Ultimately, at some time or the other, Divine justice plays its role and settles the *karmic* accounts of everybody with total impartiality.

106. Live one day at a time; don't rush

Divide your life into days and then try to live and enjoy one day at a time. Shut out all yesterdays and all tomorrows. Then you will have only one day's problems to conquer and anybody can overcome just one day's problems. It is only when you add yesterday's problems and tomorrow's apprehensions into today's burdens that it becomes unbearable for you to handle. ***It is only by dividing your life into small units that you can put your whole mind into it without distraction of past and future and get enjoyment out of it. When your mind simultaneously moves into past and future, it can't perform the present task well.***

You can even divide your day further into hours and minutes and then live and enjoy each minute separately forgetting every other thing. This is the key to joy as well as success.

107. Slow down the speed of your mind

Minds of most of the people run with a tremendous velocity with one thought after another. Their minds are not able to be still even for a moment. They are always planning, worrying, moving and tensing. Gradually, it becomes a deep rooted habit and a type of mindset. Even when there is nothing to worry, these people search some cause for worry and remain under free-floating anxiety. When there is nothing to do, they become tense as to what to do now instead of utilizing this opportunity to relax their minds.

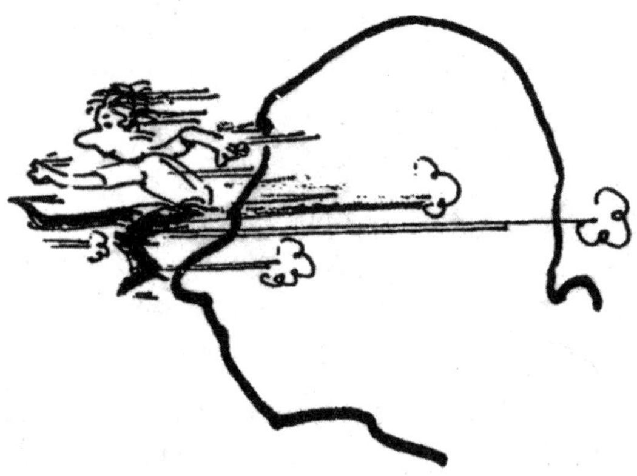

What is meant by high velocity of mind? It is a parameter indicating the number of thoughts moving across your mind per unit of time. ***Slowing down your mind essentially means reducing the number of thoughts*** **crossing your mind per unit of time.** Suppose previously one thousand thoughts used to move across your mind in a minute and now only a hundred thoughts move at the same time; it means you have slowed down your mind to that extent. Velocity of mind is particularly high during all negative emotions and stress and significantly high during emotions of impatience, hurry and desperation.

High velocity of mind or the tremendous rush of thoughts in mind is essentially a sign of weak and uncontrolled mind. A controlled mind can continue to keep only one thought for as long as it desires without allowing other thoughts to come in. It may even remain thoughtless for a period of time it desires.

Now the way to reduce the velocity of mind is to slow it down to attend to only the present activity in your hands. Don't remain in the memory of past and anticipations and apprehensions of future. Learn to live in the present. ***It is only when you think ahead of time and become past and future oriented that the speed of your mind increases*** and it also leads to poor performance of the present task in hand.

Normally, while doing anything, we think ahead of the time when this work will be finished and we can enjoy our leisure. In this process, we neglect the present and spend our time right now in unhappiness. It is our future oriented and rushing mind which blocks our happiness of the present moment and keeps our mind constantly agitated.

Once you learn to slow down your mind to the activity in hand, you will find that the most ordinary and mundane works, which earlier used to be quite boring, become quite interesting and a source of great joy and satisfaction.

It is only by slowing down and paying attention to each moment that many of the things happening around us, which are normally taken for granted and seem dull and uninteresting, become highly interesting and enjoyable. If we want to experience joy and happiness in our works, we should leave the attitude of rushing through our activities and to somehow finish them as early as possible. This should be replaced by an attitude of care and awareness in each activity, however trivial it may be. If we are not mindful in each small activity, we can't be mindful in carrying out big tasks also because attitude and frame of mind can't be suddenly changed.

108. Does your conversation often end in irritation and heart burning?

Normally, it is seen that although people start their conversation with all good intentions, but, after some time, it is found that the scene has changed. A sort of leg pulling has started, where each one is only interested in establishing his superiority over the other, rather than in the exchange of useful knowledge. This happens because people become more interested in satisfying their false ego and forget the real aim of conversation for which it was started.

If we can only remember this fact continuously in our mind during conversation that the ***primary aim of any conversation is useful exchange of knowledge and not the establishment of one's superiority over the other, we will probably save ourselves from much heart burning which is the end of many conversations***. Inspite of all your precautions, if you feel that any discussion is leading towards irritation, it is wise to stop it at that stage, howsoever logical your points may be. You should also ensure to involve only in productive discussions which lead to some enhancement of knowledge. If you feel that a certain discussion/argument/conversation by some person is quite unproductive and simply a time and energy waster, don't participate in it. Simply be a passive listener and go from there at the least opportunity.

Also, if you feel out of tune in talking with some person, then reduce your talking with him as much as possible instead of ending up everytime in tension, irritation and heart burning.

109. Cope with one problem at a time

We all know that we are surrounded by umpteen number of problems. If we start thinking and tackling all the problems at the same time, we will become mad and won't be able to solve even one problem properly. The correct approach is that you make a list of all your problems and then take out one problem at a time and then just concentrate on that problem. Shut out all other problems temporarily. By coping with one problem at a time, you will find the problem not overwhelming, but, stimulating. You will feel the enjoyment of problem-solving adventure. ***It is only when you look at and try to solve all the problems simultaneously that you get overwhelmed by them.***

110. Don't leave your mind idle

Some people spend their lifetime as if they have to somehow pass the time of their life by indulging in any kind of work. It appears that their purpose is just to die one day. But you must understand that this life is very precious. It has not been given to us for wasting it in useless and aimless pursuits. ***We have not come on this earth for a vacation.*** We have to achieve some purpose here.

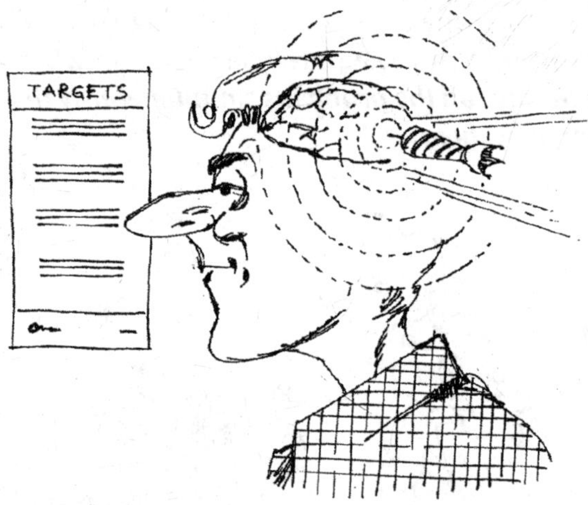

Mind should always have some goal.

Leading life aimlessly is like kicking a football in the field here and there without aiming it towards the goal of the other party. You must make some short term and long term goals in your professional as well as personal life and then systematically work to achieve them step by step. All these short term and long term goals will finally become the basis of attaining the highest aim of life which is ***Self-realization***. Whatever you think, speak or do, there must be some aim. Aimless pursuits are discouraged in yoga. ***A directionless mind normally succumbs to its lower nature and becomes the victim of all types of vices and lower instincts.***

111. Don't imagine problems and mishappenings in life

Some persons waste lot of their time in imagining many future problems, i.e., lest this or that should happen to them. In this connection, please remember that problems and adverse happenings in life should be just faced as and when they come. One should not constantly dwell and focus on possible future mishappenings which may fall upon a person. For example, don't think that "what will happen if I get cancer?"; "what will happen if my children leave me alone in old age?" or "what will happen if I lose my job?" And so on. In fact, you will find that ***ninety-nine percent of things you imagine never take place. They are just the construction of your doubtful mind and wild imagination.***

As mentioned earlier, ***even if some mishap happens, you always have the power to handle it. No problem or mishappening can be greater than you.*** Further, you are never left alone in any adversity. Omniscient and Almighty God is always with you in whatever situation you may be. ***The whole world may leave you, but He will never leave you.*** So never lose heart and always remember this principle: ***'Just face the problems as they come. Don't dwell and brood over them.'***

112. Don't stop your life when you are upset

Many people stop or at least slow down their life when they are upset. Your mood may have been upset either by some annoying remarks by somebody or by some insult or bitter sarcasm somewhere or due to failure in some project and so on. There may be a thousand and one reasons.

Till your mood becomes normal, all your life activities go in a slow pace. We don't realise that by stopping or slowing our works because of our bad mood, we are further escalating the damage by loss of precious time during which our life is stopped or slowed down.

Sooner or later, when our mood becomes normal, our life is again going to catch the pace, but, loss of time in the transition period is a loss forever. That time can never be brought back. The point is that life can't be stopped. It has to move on. Sooner or later, you have to regain your normal speed of work, so why to disturb it at all during that short period? You may say it is not practically possible, but force yourself by the use of will-power and try not to disturb the tempo of your work during the bad mood period realizing that it will be a double loss. Even if your mood doesn't cooperate, still let the work go on. In fact, keeping yourself busy during the bad mood period also helps you in the sense that your mind doesn't go to that negative incident again and again.

As far as your mood is concerned, you will, in any case, forget that particular annoying incident by the next week, next month or next year because of the rush of many new events which will dilute the effect of the earlier annoying incidents. So why not forget the unpleasant incident as early as possible and restore your mood to normal?

113. Avoid constant bickerings and complaints

Some people have the habits of constant bickering and complaining, e.g. "this is not done; that is not right; I don't like this; I don't like that; people haven't asked me before doing this or that" etc., etc. The list is endless. Their bag is always full of complaints about people and situation. These people seldom appreciate the good things. In fact, anything done well just doesn't bother them. They forget the good things quickly. Their emphasis is only on the negative side of life. Only complaints, and complaints. Because of this attitude, they constantly remain under tension. This is because you can always make an endless list of lapses in any human performance since no human being is perfect.

Instead of constant bickering in irritation, you should bring about some changes in your attitude and response. First of all, learn to appreciate the good things done by any person. Secondly, whenever you have to point out any shortcoming in a certain thing to a person, then point it out objectively, preferably in writing, if it is pertaining to the official work as if it is a natural thing and can be remedied. Don't become emotional about it. There shouldn't be any personal grudge or ill will against that person. However, attempt should be made to mend a person first by psychological means using your managerial and behavioural skills.

In case you have a complaint against somebody who is not your subordinate, but your equal or superior or a person of other department, then only request instead of spoiling relations with him by converting the issue into personal fight. However, if they don't bother, write to their higher authorities. Experience in life shows that changing your tone into tone of request and expressing your views smilingly instead of showing sign of irritation, often works wonders in getting things done from others. ***Please remember that your purpose in this life is not to set various people right or to take revenge against bad people for their behaviour. All these works relating to justice and controlling the overall world order belong to God. Your objective is simply to get your works done by crossing through the barriers (in the form of persons and situations) in such a way that minimum of resentment, violence, anger and confrontation arises. Please note that howsoever bad a person may be, but, confrontation and quarrels are never the ways to cross through him.*** You may search many other diplomatic ways and tactics to tackle him. ***To get irritated over non-agreeable person and situations is not an act of bravery and greatness. Anybody can do it.*** Your greatness lies in rising above such mechanical behaviour by asserting control on yourself.

You should be sometimes even ready to face insults and compromise with the misbehaviour of others in the larger interest of getting a good work done because that work is more important for you than a person's behaviour.

Also learn to set the things right by yourself instead of only bothering as to whose fault it is and who should correct it. Of course, you can inform the concerned person (after setting the things right) so that he becomes aware of his lapse. Even you can also take some action against the person for not being sincere in his duties.

114. Don't waste your energy in pleasing & satisfying others

Some people make Herculean efforts to please and satisfy others, but these people end up being a frustrated lot when, in the long run, they find that all their efforts have gone futile and nobody has really been satisfied.

In fact, ***proceeding in such type of mission is like making a fool of oneself because the truth is that what to say of all, you can't satisfy even a single person.*** The reason being that everybody is a bundle of countless expectations and desires and it is impossible to satisfy all the expectations of a person. If there is anybody you can satisfy, it is only yourself and not anybody else. In a similar way, any other person can be satisfied only by himself and not by anybody else.

So, don't waste time and energy unnecessarily in trying to please and satisfy others. ***Trying always lead to tension. Happiness is a natural and effortless state of mind. Happiness can't be given or transmitted to others by force.*** When your mind is calm and quiet and free from all negative emotions, you automatically experience happiness. Happiness is not an object which can be given to somebody. It is a feeling which one has to experience within himself. ***The greatest contribution you can make in making other people happy is that you first make yourself happy and cheerful so that vibrations emitted by you induce a similar state in others.***

115. Avoid excessive thinking and planning

Some people waste lot of their time in thinking and thinking. They do lot of planning in their imagination and continuously think that they want to do this and that. Although their intentions are not bad and they really want to learn and achieve something in life, but they are not able to achieve what they want because their approach is not correct. They remain all the time in frustration and depression for not achieving what they want. **This is because most of their time is lost in thinking. Even when they actually work, their mind remains on thinking about future.** So they are not able to concentrate even in their present work properly.

Although certain amount of thinking and planning is very necessary for doing a job perfectly, it is the constant inner chatter going in the mind which is not desirable. The best way to stop this inner chatter and achieve maximum in life is that **never allow yourself idling and day-dreaming for a long time.** Always take up something (from your big list of works) and get absorbed in it. Then take up another and get involved in it. Your frustration comes from the fact that you want to do and achieve everything instantly or in the least possible time. This, as you know, is mathematically impossible. Moreover you also know that your desires, your plans also keep on changing as a function of time. For example, your desires and plans are not the same as you had twenty years ago. At that time (twenty years ago), you were so desperate about certain things, but, now you are not.

That's why, as mentioned before, you have not to wait for some later date for your enjoyment when all your plans will materialize. You should derive enjoyment right in the process of work by remaining completely focussed in each work and activity which will lead to the fulfilment of your final goal. **Your enjoyment depends on your ability to remain in the present moment while doing any activity and to perform that activity as best as you can.**

116. Don't try to change others

If we closely examine our life, we will discover that most of our energy is wasted in trying to change others. We never stop to think even for a moment as to whether we also need to be changed. **We always think that others are responsible for sorrow and misery in our life and unless others change, we can't be happy.**

The hard fact of life is that you can't change others directly and forcefully. Rather, the more force you apply to change others, the more their ego becomes adamant not to change because it is the characteristic of ego to oppose or to resist. Ego can't easily say 'yes' or 'I agree'.

Change in others can only happen indirectly and can't be directly done as mentioned earlier. So, it is a happening and not a doing. Now the most important question is how to make it happen. To make it happen, the only way is to change yourself and to change your reactions and responses towards others. If you change your reaction and attitude, the other person can't continue to behave in the same fashion. He will also have to change his reaction and that is how people around you indirectly start changing by your changing.

Now, to make some change heppen in those persons who aren't directly associated with you but are working in some other public dealing departments and to whom people approach for getting their various works done, you can follow a different approach. The way is not to accuse them day and night but to write letters to appropriate authorities and occasionally meet them in small groups and apprise them of your problems, and insincerity on the part of their subordinates, if any. This will definitely bring some results, even if not to your entire satisfaction. But if you simply sit idle and only accuse and abuse these people amongst yourselves, nothing will happen except that you will go on building tension and frustration inside.

In spiritual life, your aim is not to change bad persons and remove badness from the world. Important thing is how you react to the badness so that:

i) Damage to you and surroundings due to this badness is minimized.

ii) You don't give energy from your side to aggravate and increase the existing badness further. Rather you starve it by withdrawing energy and food to it. Existing badness can only increase if you provide fuel and energy to it. This way, you indirectly contribute in reduction of badness in the environment.

You may also devise ways of dealing with others by your intelligence and diplomacy so that their badness doesn't get a chance to arise and originate in the first place. In these ways, you allow badness to die its own death without having to fight with it.

So the bottom line is that ***"the only way to change others is to change yourself and your reaction towards others."***

117. Be lavish in praise but miser in criticism

We are very miserly when it comes to praising others for their good things. But we are very prompt when it comes to fault finding and pointing out shortcomings and mistakes in other's works. We should try to develop the opposite attitude, that we should praise lavishly whenever we find any good thing in

anyone and for any good work done by someone. This gives encouragement and support to the person for continuing and carrying forward his good things further. On the other hand, we should be miserly in publicizing the defects and shortcomings of others. There is a quotation **"praise in public and criticize in private."** It doesn't mean that you shouldn't do anything after noticing the faults, mistakes, shortcomings in a certain thing committed by a certain person. If a person is working under you and you want to point out some defect, shortcoming or deficiency to him, you should call him in private and point out in person. But you should never advertise somebody's faults and weaknesses in public.

It is also to be noticed that whenever you focus on negative points of a person, you are also temporarily charged with negativity and whenever you think of positive points, you are temporarily charged with positivity. So, you can realize that it is also in your own benefit to focus more on positive points of others rather than negative points.

Another thing we should realize is that only a person who works can commit mistakes. We see many people who themselves will not do anything but if anybody takes initiative, they will always be on the lookout to search points for criticizing him, to look for any shortcomings and deficiencies in his work, to look for any slips or lapses by him to trap him somewhere. This is not a spiritual and mature attitude. Mature attitude is to give positive support to a person if he is showing some initiative.

118. Develop more & more *Satoguna*

Our *yogic* texts and ancient scriptures talk about three types of tendencies or *gunas* in the constitution of man, namely:

(i) Rajoguna
(ii) Satoguna
(iii) Tamoguna

While *rajoguna* and *tamoguna* pull you downwards towards your lower nature, *satoguna* pulls you upwards towards your higher or divine nature. *Rajoguna* is characterized by overactive and restless mind always craving for some kind of excitement, thrill and ego based pleasures. Under the influence of *rajoguna*, although, you seem to be very active and running about a lot, but it doesn't give you any feeling of real fulfilment, upliftment and joy in life. You simply remain tense, agitated, excited and discontented.

Taking *satwik* food increases *satoguna* in you.

Tamoguna is characterized by inertia, dullness, inactivity, laziness, carelessness, procrastination. You want to remain drowsy, sleepy, forgetful. It also doesn't give you any fulfilment and you feel simply dead and dull.

Satoguna is characterized by an active but serene and balanced mind. ***Satoguna* is the middle point between *rajoguna* and *tamoguna*. It contains the good points of both.** Persons with *satoguna* are neither overexcited (as in *rajoguna*) nor dull and dead (like in *tamoguna*). **They remain in a beautiful blend of activity and relaxation.** They remain active yet calm, stressfree and relaxed (meditation in action).

If we want to develop spiritually, we should grow more and more in *satoguna* or *satwa*. Our lifestyle should be *satwik* and we should try to live as much as possible in *satwik* environment. **In fact, *Satwa* acts as means to attain the ultimate goal of your life, i.e. Self-realization.** Taking *satwik* food, listening to *satwik* music, remaining close to nature, leading a regular lifestyle, maintaining cleanliness of your body and surroundings, doing regular yoga, *pranayama*, meditation, maintaining silence as much as possible, using soothing and spiritual colours in your surroundings, installing elevating photos and pictures in your surroundings, using natural objects as far as possible instead of synthetic materials, study of soul elevating literature are all efforts in the direction of strengthening *satoguna* inside you.

119. Don't damage yourself while serving others

There is great misunderstanding in our society regarding the word '**service**'. People normally think that a person is great if he damages and sacrifices himself in serving and helping others. But spirituality doesn't encourage such mindless phenomena.

Take due precautions to protect yourself while serving a patient.

As per spiritual philosophy, you must help others, do whatever service you can do for the welfare of society and others but not by damaging yourself. If you destroy yourself, how will you serve others? You have to keep yourself physically and mentally fit in order to help and serve others properly. I have seen many persons who while serving a sick and infected patient do not take proper precautions to protect themselves in the name of love and care and catch his disease and infection.

Bearing some inconvenience and discomfort and doing some extra physical labour in serving others to the capacity of the body is all right but harming and destroying yourself in the process is not a sign of wisdom and maturity. The right way of help is doing service while keeping yourself mentally and physically fit and strong. Some people may call it selfishness but this is not. The real meaning of selfishness is doing something for yourself while harming others or ignoring the interest of others. ***Doing something for your protection, development and comforts without harming and affecting anyone is not selfishness.***

Of course, on some rare occasions, sacrificing yourself for the sake of others may be appropriate only when it is for the larger interest of mankind and society and serves some bigger cause or purpose. This is because 'whole' is always important than the 'part'. But sacrificing for any Tom, Dick & Harry and for petty things & attachments is not a desirable thing from the spiritual perspective.

120. Learn to accept everything in life

One of the major causes of sorrow and tension in our lives is that we are not able to accept if something unfavourable, bad, unexpected occurs to us in life. Suppose we have failed in an examination or we have contracted a disease or somebody close to us has cheated us. In these conditions we become highly tense and frustrated as to why it happened. Our thoughts run like this *"I had never expected it; I worked so hard still I failed; I did so much for that person, still he cheated; Why people do not cooperate with me and attend to me properly."*

The key to happiness is that you change your mental attitude from resistance to acceptance. You should affirm in your mind that ***"I will accept everything in life no matter what happens, good or bad, pleasant or unpleasant. I realize that anything can happen in life."*** Since both good and bad persons are there in this world, so both good and bad things can happen. Even a good person can turn into a bad person and a bad person can turn into a good person later on. There should be no surprise in it. All possibilities are open in life.

For solution of any problem, the first step is acceptance, i.e. this problem is there and it could be there. There is nothing unusual in the existence of this problem. And the second step is to find remedial measures or to make efforts in the direction of overcoming the problem. But if you are not able to take the first step, how will you take the second step?

121. Don't develop hatred for the bad

We are taught from the very beginning of life "Love the good and hate the bad." And logically it seems justified also that if a thing is bad, why should we not hate it. So we gradually start accumulating hatred in our hearts towards all bad things/ persons/events we come across in life. But true spirituality doesn't advocate this principle. ***Spirituality teaches us that don't hate any thing or any person no matter how bad or mean he is.***

The reason being that by hating a bad thing , you are neither helping that thing nor yourself. By hating a bad thing or person, it is not going to change. Similarly, you harm yourself because your mind becomes negatively charged whenever you hate, and this harms you both mentally and physically as your mind and body are linked.

Hatred is never a right relationship with anything because once you hate a thing, you become attached to it in terms of hatred. You are not able to let it go from your mind. That thing revolves around your mind continuously. ***Spirituality advocates detachment both from good and bad.*** It wants you to be simply an observer of both good and bad and attached to neither of them. So if you hate a thing , how will you develop detachment which is the very key to spirituality?

The right approach to deal with the bad is not to see it with the eyes of hatred but to accept it, first of all, and then ponder over the causes which have led to this state. And then decide what contribution you can make in diluting or dissolving that badness. It is true that you can't change every bad thing into good thing in this world and it is not expected also. Only whatever little is possible within your power and limitations, you are supposed to make full use of it. ***It is not necessary to take a pledge to root out all the badness from the world.***

In short, instead of hating, put your energy in taking action to improve upon a thing, if it is bad, to whatever extent possible. However, there are many things in life which are beyond your control. In such situations, instead of cursing yourself and others, accept them as your fate and adjust yourself in such a manner that the harm caused from a bad thing to you is minimum. ***In other words, when you can't do anything outwardly, just change your reaction or response towards that thing.***

122. Don't make others dependent and handicapped

It is generally seen that in the name of respect and pleasing others, people generally don't allow others especially elders to do their work by themselves. *In spirituality, the principle is that help should be given when it is really needed, otherwise we are making that person dependent and handicapped* and not allowing him to develop his own powers and confidence to meet the challenges and demands of life. In other words , one should deserve the help which is being given to him and help should not be wasted.

It is often seen in our traditional families that if an elderly person does something by himself, e.g. takes water by himself or puts his used utensils at a proper place, we won't allow him to do that and we think it is a sign of great respect. But we don't realise that by doing this we are gradually making him handicapped and eroding his self-confidence.

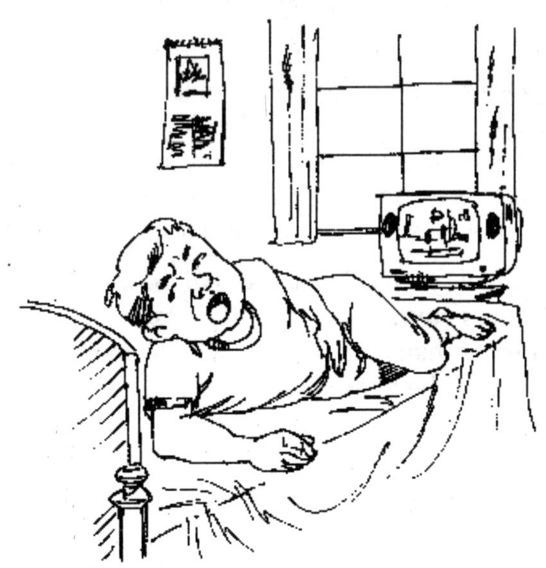

Encourage your children to do their works by themselves.

As per spiritual philosophy, whatever work you can do by yourself, you must do it by yourself and should not look for others to do it for you. ***Help should be asked only when it is really needed.*** This principle applies to persons of all ages and older persons are not immune to this rule. True, older persons can do fewer things by themselves compared to the young but those little chores should be done by themselves and this should not be confused with loss of respect and dignity. The feeling in our culture that it is a sign of respect that elderly persons should not be allowed to do anything by themselves and all their works should be done by others is not based on right thinking.

In many households where servants are employed, it is often seen that children are ordering servants to do small small things for them which they can easily do by themselves. This attitude becomes an ideal setting for making them dependent and handicapped in future and suffer thereby because everywhere and every time, they will not have persons around to work for them. ***We should encourage children to do as much work by themselves as possible and the habit of spoon-feeding to them should be avoided as much as possible.***

The age-old quotation that ***"God helps those who help themselves"*** has much to teach us in this regard. Its hidden meaning is that once you start doing anything by yourself, then God and other forces of the universe also start supporting you by various means. But if you don't do even what you can do , then one must not rely on God also.

In spiritual philosophy also, ***a real master is said to be one who produces masters and not followers,*** imitators and disciples dependent on him. His aim remains to make everybody as independent as he himself is.

123. Go beyond prejudices and biases

We easily develop prejudices and biases for various things in life because of not seeing things in their totality and forming opinion by seeing only one side or face of a situation/person/thing or because of our preconceived beliefs and conditioning. Our prejudices take the following shapes:

1. If someone has done something good or pleasant to you, you become biased in his favour and everywhere you start supporting him whether right or wrong. Similarly, if someone has done or said something bad to you, then you become biased against him and you start opposing him in everything whether right or wrong.

Getting biased with a particular group or community is an obstacle against your growth.

2. You generalize things based on seeing one attribute of a person. Suppose you have seen some good aspect of a person. Now as a biased person you will generalize that this person has all good points in him though actually

it may not be so. Similarly, if you have seen some bad point in a person, you generalize that he is through and through a bad person, though this may not be so. He may have some good points also which you may not have come across.

You also generalize on a larger level also. For example, if a person of some community has done a bad action, then we generalize the whole community as bad. Similarly, suppose you follow a certain faith/religion, then you get biased in favour of it and every time you try to justify all its preachings, whether rational or not, and you consider its preachings superior as compared to other religions/faiths.

3. You tend to exaggerate things based on one observation. For example, you may see one bad action of somebody and exaggerate it beyond proportion. You don't see the full picture before exaggerating things. You don't collect facts and proper details before giving conclusions and your opinions. You tend to have fragmented and partial vision. Spreading rumours against somebody because of incomplete and fragmented information also comes under the same tendency.

Spirituality teaches us to remain impartial, detached and not to be carried away by one aspect of a thing. It exhorts us to see things in totality by observing all the facts and pros & cons related to a thing and only then make any conclusion about it. This is where our rational and analytical faculty (intellect) comes into picture. To become hateful and repulsive against a thing or to be too much attached to a thing, both are extremes. Spirituality teaches us to remain in the middle by carefully weighing everything rationally and holistically.

124. Don't exploit the weak and helpless

It is frequently observed that the persons who are superior to you in power and money, you remain humble and submissive to them while persons who are weak monetarily or otherwise and working under you, your attitude towards them is of dominating and exploiting nature. Instead of helping such persons to rise upwards and come out of their limitations, you rather try to exploit them for your selfish gains because you know that you can force them to succumb to your unreasonable demands and they will not resist because of their compulsion and helplessness.

This attitude of exploitation of the weak and helpless is the sign of lower level of consciousness and will not help you to grow spiritually. You should also keep in mind that no matter how much you torture or exploit the weak here on this earth

Torturing the weak and helpless is very inhuman.

because of your apparent superiority in wealth, power and connections, ***but in the God's account books, you will have to settle each and every agony you have inflicted on others***. There is no concession there and no weightage of your influential position on earth. In His kingdom, all are treated alike - whether rich or poor, powerful or weak. The basis of judgement there is your character, behaviour and your divine qualities and not your material status.

Further, remember that external differences of status, power and wealth are only temporary and can anytime swing from this side to that side based on the changing destiny. They don't indicate real superiority or inferiority.

125. Don't be obsessed with external rituals & worships

We, Indians, remain very much engrossed in external worship and rituals. Though not wrong by itself, it becomes counterproductive when it becomes the end of your spiritual practice and no more remains the means. If you use them as symbols to pay your adoration, salutation and glorification of the Supreme, then there is no harm. *Problem comes when you continuously remain limited to and obsessed with these concrete forms of worship and don't go beyond it and expand yourself.* If you remain limited to idol worship and consider God residing only in the idol and in the temple, then you have not taken the advantage which temples and outer rituals/ worships offer to you.

External worship should not become the end in itself.

Temple is only a symbol for the abode of God, so that whenever you see temple, it makes you remember God (at least in the initial stages). Similarly, all rituals/external forms of worship are symbols for awakening in you the feeling of adoration and admiration of that great Being (God) to whom the whole universe and its inhabitants are subservient and owe their very existence. Whenever you worship, adore and admire a great being, you yourself are purified.

A temple (including church, mosque, *gurudwara* or any place of worship) also provides you a place which is filled with positive energy and vibrations because it is normally ensured that everything being used in these places is *satwik* and pure. It is also assumed that people visiting temples keep their minds positive and don't harbour any negative thoughts, at least temporarily, while inside the temple. In the construction of many temples, even the principles of *Vaastu* (our ancient and valuable science) are also fully taken care of in the form of placement of various things with due regard to directions and the five elements. Chanting of devotional music, sounds of temple bells & conches and regular *satsangs* further elevate the atmosphere of the temple. All this makes the environment full of positive energy and vibrations and benefits us when we are inside the temple.

You should take full advantage of this atmosphere to elevate yourself but you should not stop yourself here but should finally proceed to to your real goal which is "Self-realization or God-realization" or in other words to go inside in your inner temple and enjoy the real and permanent bliss abiding there. When you come to this state, you are able to sense God everywhere and not in the temple alone. You always move in the state of God-consciousness and see His hand and *leela* in everything.

126. Don't torture your body by false penance

There have been various religious sects and cults in our country who teach their followers/sanyasins/monks/nuns to renounce worldly pleasures and comforts and to abhor them. They even claim that it is a sin to give pleasure and comforts to *Indriyas* (senses) of the body. They call it *Bhoga* and they advise that *indriyas* or senses should be deprived and starved of their pleasures. Only then they can remain pure and in control. Some have gone to the extent of torturing their bodies and *indriyas* in the name of penance (*Tapasya*) e.g. standing in scorching heat and freezing cold, standing on one foot for days together, walking barefoot on thorns, sleeping on a bed of thorns, starving the body without food, standing in ice freeze water etc. They claim that by giving such suffering and torture to the body, they will be cleansed of their sins and will attain God quickly.

Torturing body by false penance doesn't lead to good results.

Nothing can be farther from truth. If pleasures and comforts were undesirable for the body, God would not have given appropriate senses in our body to enjoy them at the first place. In fact, suppression of natural pleasures and comforts can be disastrous for your body. It may lead to unnecessary perversions and various psychological problems. Please note that that the word 'Control'(or *Samyam* in Sanskrit) in spirituality signifies mastery over *indriyas* or body and not the killing or torture of *indriyas* or body.

Now what is wrong is not the enjoyment of pleasures and comforts but attachment to them, over-indulgence/addiction to them, constant thinking and talking about them. You should enjoy them when the need and right moment is there and then let it go. You should not keep on ruminating about them in thinking and imagination. That is what attachment is.

Another thing to be kept in mind is that there are two kinds of pleasures - Lower pleasures and Higher pleasures. Lower pleasures (also known as *rajasik* and ego based pleasures) should definitely be avoided and controlled as they are harmful to the body and mind. It is only the enjoyment of Neutral and Higher pleasures we are talking about. Neutral pleasures are those pleasures which are related to bodily survival (e.g. satisfaction of basic needs, urges and comforts of the body).

Higher pleasures are also called *Satwik* pleasures. They are related to pure nature and its five elements (Akasha, Air, Water, Agni, Earth). The more your life-style is close to nature, the more *satwik* you are. *Satwik* pleasures calm down and steady your mind and help you to elevate spiritually.

Note: To know more about *Satwik, Rajasik, Tamsik* and ego based pleasures, please refer chapters 18 and 62 in my book **"77 Lessons to Remain Ever Positive".**

127. Don't be an imitator or a follower

We, Indians, have a great tendency to be followers of some sect or religion or *guru* or faith or some institution and we feel proud that we are a follower of such and such cult. And we feel astonished if somebody says that he is not a follower of anything and is an independent being.

Please remember that if you want to blindly follow and imitate somebody or some institution or some religious precept, you can never become enlightened and attain freedom (or *Mukti* in the language of our scriptures) which is the ultimate

A follower can't taste the real bliss.

goal of spirituality. A real *guru* or master does not encourage blind following and rather warns of the dangers of imitation no matter how enlightened a master may be. In fact, it is said that a real *guru* produces *gurus* and masters like himself and not a crowd of followers and disciples. Followers are like a herd of sheep who have lost their own soul and just want to follow somebody blindly so that they don't have to think and exert at all as to what and why they are doing. If you turn the pages of history, you will find that the real genius and great persons were not followers of anybody or anything but had made their own path. Only a person with independent personality can taste the real freedom and bliss of life.

If you really want to be spiritual, you should be a learner and not a follower, i.e. you must learn from the our great lineage of our thinkers, sages, saints but then make your own path and plan for progress by utilizing this learning and mixing your own thinking and contemplation in it. But saying that you believe in something because it is written in some religious scripture or has been uttered by a famous *guru* having millions of followers is not a scientific and responsible statement. Your own potential of greatness is not less than any great person who has ever been on this earth. Even if a thing is absolutely right, you must try to understand and experience it by yourself instead of accepting blindly. ***A borrowed knowledge, however correct it may be, doesn't do much good to anyone***. You should also have the courage to discard those things which you don't find scientific and practicable. It is not necessary that preachings of a religion or *guru* will be hundred percent correct and scientific.

This is the basic principle of spirituality: **"Learn from everybody. Respect everybody. But don't follow or attach to anybody. Follow only yourself"**.